When Football Was Fun

Bert Mozley

The Breedon Books Publishing Company

First published in Great Britain by
The Breedon Books Publishing Company Limited
Breedon House, 44 Friar Gate, Derby, DE1 1DA.
1999

ISBN 1 85983 187 7

Printed and bound by Butler & Tanner Ltd.,
Selwood Printing Works, Caxton Road, Frome, Somerset.
Cover printed by Lawrence Allen Colour Printers, Gazelle Road, Weston-super-Mare, Avon.

Contents

Early Days

SOME of the happiest days of my life were spent playing football on Chester Green. I was born on 23 September 1923 at home, 33 Old Chester Road in Derby. My Dad, awaiting the birth and hoping for a daughter, was talking in the yard to our neighbour Mrs Stannard The nurse opened the upstairs window and shouted, "Mr Mozley, you have a daughter." Dad duly received congratulations and continued to talk, but 15 minutes later the window opened again and the nurse was shouting, "Mr Mozley, you have a son." At this point Dad looked at Mrs Stannard and said, "I think I'd better go inside before any more come along."

My brother Cliff, who was almost two years old at the time, didn't take very kindly to the new babies and wanted to know when they were 'going back home'. He had been the centre of attention and didn't like the idea of sharing his parents with us at all.

From what I have been told, from the time that I was able to walk, I was always kicking something. If not a ball, then a stone or a piece of wood. Anything that was on the floor in front of me, I would attempt to kick. My Mum had to tie a piece of white tape around my right shoe – 'like the footballers' – and I guess I wouldn't go out, even in the pushchair, until she had done this. I must have known that my right foot was my best kicking foot even at that early age.

Our back garden led out to an entry and as we were too young to play in the street, Cliff and I would kick the ball to each other. We had a tennis ball and would try to pass it without touching the sides of the entry which was only about three feet wide. He would stand at one end and me at the other. I guess in some small way this helped me to master place kicking – but it certainly didn't help the toes on our shoes! My first pair of 'footers' was an old pair of black boots. My Dad bought some cogs (now called studs) and nailed these on to the soles. To me the sound of those studs as they hit the pavement was the best sound in the world I really felt grown up. I believe I was around four years old at the time.

As we grew older and were allowed to play outside, it was always football. At that time there was a railway bridge over the top of Old Chester Road, so when it was wet we were still able to play under the bridge and stay dry. We would chalk goalposts up on each side of the brick walls and then pick sides.

I remember some of those names from the 1930s. There was Fred Beeson, my brother Cliff, the Clarke brothers – Herbert and Bill – and my cousin Ron

Mum and Dad – Charlie and Edie Mozley.

Woodward, (who unfortunately lost his life at a very early age with the Parachute Brigade over Arnhem, in World War Two). The rest of the 'gang' comprised of the Grimadell brothers, Albert Smith, Albert Coulson and.

Harold Kellet (who also lost his life in an accident when in the RAF). Sid Strelley and Jack Campbell were friends of my brother but we younger kids were allowed to make up the team if they were short of a player. We were all

Twins...Beryl and me, Girl Guide and Boy Scout.

from working class families and to own a real football was unheard of. There was one boy, I believe his name was Mason, who was the owner of such a prize and you can bet there were a lot of knocks on Mason's door to see if he could come out to play – as long as he brought the ball out with him!

I know there were others, but these are the ones that I remember so well. We would play for hours – come rain or shine and as TV was unheard of at that time – and there wasn't a single fat kid in the group!

It wasn't long after I started school, at St Paul's on Mansfield Street, that I was picked to play for the school team. I must confess that I didn't pay as much attention to the three R's as I should – but I just couldn't wait for playtime so that we could play football. I remember the day when I fell in the schoolyard and banged my face. There wasn't time to stop playing as my side was losing and it wasn't until I went to get a drink of cold water, that I realised I had chipped my two front teeth. I can still feel that pain when the cold water hit the nerve end!

St Paul's was lucky to have Mr Morley as the sports master. He was a good coach and we had a pretty good team. When I was ten years old I was selected to play for Derby Boys and although I don't remember very much about it, I'm sure it was because of the coaching I received from that gentleman. Our headmaster was Mr Hallam and we all respected him. He was fair but strict and could give a whack with the cane with his left hand and never miss a letter whilst writing with the other… (Ouch!)

Three Musketeers – big brother Cliff and me. Cliff's pal Sid Strelley is at the rear.

One Christmas time at school, we had a party and a magician came to entertain us. I remember it so well. I was sitting on the front row and he came to me and produced a half-crown from out of my nose. I guess I was about ten years old. I was so impressed that all the way walking home I kept blowing my nose until it bled, trying to get another half-crown. From that day, I have been interested in magic and even now, one of the things I always make a point of doing when I visit Derby, is to 'phone my old friend Joe Bonsall from Breadsall. Joe, who is a member of the Magic Circle, has taught me several tricks that I now entertain my own granddaughters with. On my last visit he arranged a special treat for me. He invited another Derby magician over to his house, Ian Barradell. I have watched many performers in my lifetime but this man had me mesmerised. if I could have been as good with my feet as he is with his hands – I'd be playing now.

When I was about ten years old I had two 'heroes'. One was Harry Bedford who played for Derby County and the other our local hero, Amos Brown, who played for Darley Abbey. Friday night was always 'bath night' and with hair that was wet I would ask Mum to part my hair so that I looked like Harry Bedford! Amos lived across the street and to be allowed to carry

Still prepared for anything! Beryl and me in later years.

his 'footer' boots when he was going to play on Darley Fields really made my day… real 'footer' boots! My first pair came one Christmas and I guess I wouldn't take them off all day. Probably not too good for Mum's lino – or the bed clothes either as I'm told by my sister that I slept with them still on!

I recall when St Paul's won the Derby Schoolboys Cup in 1936-37. Our home ground was, of course, on

Chester Green and the workers at Haslam's factory were some of our staunchest supporters. Most of the parents would be on hand with the oranges at half-time. Unfortunately, the final match for the Cup was to be played on a ground at Ashbourne Road, not on our home ground.

This was the first big day of my life and when we won – I remember coming home on the bus with my Mum (my best supporter) and my twin sister Beryl (who was the noisiest one) – clutching this trophy very proudly. It was a small silver cup and I think I polished it every day, as it had its special place on the mantle piece. It stayed there for quite a while, until I think I got fed up with polishing it. I still have a photograph in my gym at home with the players who took part in our 'victory' that day. I don't remember all the names but maybe someone else will. If I have omitted to mention a name – please accept my apologies, for at 75 years of age the memory doesn't work as well as it did.

As you may have guessed, I lived, breathed and slept football all the way through my school years and my big dream was that one day I would play for Derby County. I'm sure that all my team mates shared this dream too – Len Pawley, Stan Newman, Fred Beeson, John Chambers, Cliff Hall, Albert Coulson, Fred Johnson and Jimmy Young just to mention a few. I think I would have found it hard to believe then – if someone had told me – that one-day my dream would come true.

My friend Fred Beeson and I looked very much alike.

So much so that one day as we were all playing together, I got a clip at the side of the ear. Turning round I saw it was Fred's Mum looking at me and she couldn't apologise enough. Fred was late going home and I got the wallop intended for him.

There was a time when I was the envy of all my schoolmates, at least the boys. My aunt and uncle lived in Stoke and a man by the name of Bob McGrory lodged with them. Bob was the manager of Stoke City at that time.

I was invited to stay with my aunt for a week and as it happened, the Saturday that I arrived there Mr McGrory asked me if I would like to go with him to the ground to see Stoke play against Grimsby. As you can imagine this was truly a big day for me and before the game I was taken into the players' dressing room to meet them. I was introduced to Frankie Soo (who could really throw a ball in from the sideline), then to Freddie Steel who I remember was sporting two lovely black eyes acquired in a previous game. Then last, but not least, I met 'the wizard of dribble' himself, a very young Stanley Matthews. Little did I know that I would become one of the few not only who played against him many times, but also with him in the England team. I remember getting autographs and being offered the magnificent sum of sixpence from one of my pals if I'd sell one. I turned the offer down, of course (half-a-crown maybe – but not a measly 'tanner').

The year 1937 was my last at school. The leaving age

Proudly smiling behind the Derby Schoolboys Cup as skipper of the victorious St Paul's School team of 1936-37.

then was 14 and I was lucky enough to be accepted at Rolls-Royce as an apprentice. I graduated from the St Paul's School team to the Church team. All the members were around 18 and I felt very honoured to have been asked. I remember the first game that I was to play for them. It was a home game on Darley Fields and I was dressed at least two hours before the game… just couldn't wait to make my debut into the 'Big Team'.

I decided to go to the pitch and kick a few balls before the game and as I raced towards a ball and stretched to kick, I felt a sharp pain in my groin. Not knowing anything about pulled muscles at that time I was in a panic. I couldn't run – in fact I could hardly walk. Here I was, my first game with the senior side – and I couldn't play. I went home almost in tears. After this I didn't kick a ball for a long, long time. I was too scared. Many years later I was to find out that another 14-year-old had been asked to join the same side on that day too. His name was Reg Harrison. Our paths intertwined on many occasions before we finally became members of the same team.

During the next two years, I worked at Rolls-Royce and went to the Technical College for two nights each week. To get to the bus stop, I had to walk over Chester Green. One night as some kids were playing football, the ball came over to me and without giving it a thought I booted the ball back to them. I was really happy to find that there was no pain at all when I kicked. Well, that was it! Down went the books and I never did catch that bus to the Tech. What's more I'm afraid I failed to attend classes for two or three weeks until my Dad received a letter asking why I had not been. That put an end to my nightly games – but at least I had got back my love for football.

At Rolls-Royce, each year, there was an inter-shop football competition for the Claude Johnson Cup. I worked in the Experimental Department and we usually did well in this tournament. We were lucky to have some good amateur players from several clubs who played for our department. I remember Ged Thomas who signed with Nottingham Forest and Tommy Jones and George Riddell who both had signed for Derby. I remember Ron Doricott who was a good centre-half. Tom Patrick, my very good friend (who was also my best man in 1945) played alongside Ron, and to complete the half-back line was Jack Dingley. I believe George Froud played on the wing and I also remember Phil Bibby there in the forward line. We had great celebrations after the games, in the club rooms on the Osmaston Park Recreation Ground. At that time, Rolls-Royce was a good firm to work for and I was sorry to recently read that it had been sold.

Shortly after I had played for the Rolls-Royce team, I was asked by Cyril Piggins to go for a try-out with Shelton United. Cyril ran the team and the home ground was behind the Bridge Inn pub on Chellaston Road. I'm not sure if it is still there, as this was around 1942. I went one Saturday afternoon and played as an inside-forward. After this, I managed to get a regular place in the side and at the end of the season was offered amateur forms with Nottingham Forest. I played several times with them and also was allowed to continue with Shelton United.

It was after one of the Shelton games that a man by

I'm second from right on the front row of this photograph which shows the Experimental Department team which won the Rolls-Royce Inter-departmental Claude Johnson Cup in May 1944.

the name of Jack Bowers came up to me and said, "Bert, with your speed and ball distribution, you should be playing at right-back." Knowing that Jack was with Derby County, and respecting his opinion, the following week, I asked Cyril if I could change positions and try-out in defence. He told me to go ahead. It was a totally different experience but I found that I enjoyed it. I have a lot to thank those two men for. Jack Bowers for seeing something in my play that I hadn't noticed – and Cyril for letting me try out Jack's idea.

It was also while I was with Shelton United that my path crossed once again with Reg Harrison. Reg was now playing with Derby County Reserves and we were to meet them in the Final of the Bass Charity Cup.

Before the game, I went to Reg and told him not to score too many goals against us. He totally ignored me and immediately scored his hat-trick! It was after this game that he was offered a professional contract and he told me afterwards that he was paid the magnificent sum of eight pounds a week at that time.

Signing for Derby

IT was in 1944 that I got word from Derby County that I was to have a try-out with their 'A' team. It was to be played on Darley Fields. When I got there, I was told to play in the right-back position. I have to be honest in saying that I don't recall anything about that first game. I guess I was too excited to think. However, I must have done something right as I was selected for the rest of the season and offered amateur forms as well.

The following year, I was re-signed and played my first game with the Reserves. In September, which has always been a special month in my life, I finished my apprenticeship at Rolls-Royce and became an outside representative, Aero Engine Fitter. My first job was to go to the De Haviland depot at St Albans. I was to change a fuel pump. Their test pilot was Geoff De Haviland and as I was just checking over in my mind if I had done everything correctly to the 'plane, this young man in his shirt sleeves came up to me and asked me if it was finished. I must have said, "Yes," because he was in the cockpit and racing away before I could get my breath. My heart was pounding like a sledgehammer as I watched him put the plane through its test. I was thinking 'what if I installed the pump wrong?' No one was more relieved than I was, when I saw him taxi back down the runway safely. I think I got my first grey hair that day at the age of 21.

When the football season opened in 1945, I began playing regularly for the reserve team. I was offered a professional contract on 2 September and was married the day after. A great wedding present! Ted Magner was the manager then and I still remember the words he told me as I stood in his office that day. He said, "Bert, one day you will be playing before thousands of fans. All I need from you is your best effort. You have the skills and where else is there a job going that pays you to keep fit."

I never forgot his words and all my life I have tried to stay in the best of health. I still work out every day in my gym (that was once the garage). I use weights and concentrate on reps rather than heavy weightlifting. It has always been a part of my life – and will be for as long as I can manage to do it. I have to thank my sister for this interest. When we were both just 14, she was bigger than I was and I wasn't going to have that. I joined the Health and Strength organisation and read as much as I could on how to put on the pounds. I still tease her and tell her that she's bigger than I am – but only around the waist!

It wasn't long after I had signed for Derby that I

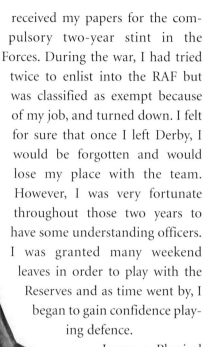

received my papers for the compulsory two-year stint in the Forces. During the war, I had tried twice to enlist into the RAF but was classified as exempt because of my job, and turned down. I felt for sure that once I left Derby, I would be forgotten and would lose my place with the team. However, I was very fortunate throughout those two years to have some understanding officers. I was granted many weekend leaves in order to play with the Reserves and as time went by, I began to gain confidence playing defence.

I was a Physical Training Instructor and was able to keep fit quite easily, as part of each day was spent out on the football field. During my training, I met Arnie Grace who was also on Derby's

Playing for the Rams. Just look at those heavy leather boots.

books. We were on a course together at one time. I believe Arnie played with the Rams reserve team but later joined the Derby police force and was a well-known local footballer for many years.

During the time that I served with the RAF I was chosen to play for the national side several times and was made captain of the team. It was a great honour but I recall one week, when I played four times in five days – twice for Derby in the FA Cup games against Chelsea and twice for the RAF side. This was the only time that I recall being leg weary and I was glad to get back to camp for a rest.

One of the RAF representative games took us to Ireland where we played against Munster in Cork. The Munster FA was celebrating its 25th anniversary. We were taken on a trip to 'kiss the blarney stone' and, as I remarked afterwards to the team, you need the luck to survive the ordeal! Someone holds your feet while you hang more or less upside down in order to kiss the stone. As I was one of the heaviest on the team, I was glad when they dragged me up and away from the sheer drop down below the stone.

As we were making our way back to the boat to return to England, we had to pass through Customs. We had all bought goods that we knew we would have to pay duty on. The officer in charge said to us, "Well lads, just do as I do and you will all be OK. Don't try to hide anything – you must declare everything you bought."

Well, he went first and was assessed and had to pay.

The Mayor of Cork meets the RAF XI which played Munster. I am the player extreme left, leaning forward behind the Mayor's left shoulder.

With the RAF in Ireland at the end of the war. On sightseeing duty outside Blarney Castle.

Then we all followed. The duty officer gave the first lad the wink and said, "If you only have one pair of silk stockings you can just walk through." Naturally, we all walked through. The officer was quite upset. I wonder why.

Another incident that sticks out in my mind when I recall my RAF days at Compton-Bassett, was the time I was told to take 80 German prisoners to another camp. They were waiting to be repatriated and were to be moved to a camp outside Birmingham. I was the sergeant in charge and after lining them all up and checking names, we left by train to go to London. We then had to transfer to another train to get to Birmingham. When we got to Reading, the train slowed down and for some reason, shunted the last coach off to another siding. As we gathered speed again I was in a real flap, as looking

Ready for the off...the team which met Munster to celebrate the 25th anniversary of the local FA.

out of the window, I could see the carriage, with half of my prisoners grinning and waving to me, left behind on the track. Well, I didn't know what to do. I could see the newspaper headlines: 'Mozley, Derby County's right-back, loses 50 prisoners-of-war.' As soon as we arrived in London, I called the Military Police right away. They said they would contact Reading for me. All the way to Birmingham, I was very uncomfortable, wondering how long I'd be in jail if any of them went missing. You can imagine my relief when on arriving at Birmingham, I was greeted with loud clapping from the 50 prisoners and a lot of laughter when they saw the state I was in. After a roll call, I was able to breathe easily once more as they were all present and correct!

Jack Nicholas was Derby's captain and right-back and had been for many years. I knew that I might have to wait for a long time before I would get the chance to take his place. It happened sooner than I thought, however. By this time manager Ted Magner had left Derby to go and coach abroad, and Stuart McMillan had taken over.

Stuart had played some games for Wolves when they won the Third Division North in 1923-24 and had appeared once for the Rams as well as playing a few games of cricket for Derbyshire. His father had enjoyed a better career and scored 50 goals for the Rams in the 1890s. Stuart was licensee of the Nag's Head at Mickleover and was acting in an advisory capacity to Derby County when Ted Magner left and he inherited a team that was on its way to winning the FA Cup for the only time in the Rams' history.

I recall Stuart calling me to the office as I reported at the weekend and telling me that Jack Nicholas was down with the 'flu and that I was to play in his place. Now that game I do remember! We were playing Preston North End at home. It was 2 November 1946 and Derby had had a moderate start to that first peacetime season, win-ning only four of their first 11 games. Actually, Jack had been injured after only three games that season but now he was fit – he was ill! So Jack Parr, another local lad who had been covering for Jack, moved to left-back and I was to make my debut in the number-two shirt.

It was all a bit complicated because Leon Leuty was also sidelined and so Jack Howe, who had been playing left-back, moved to centre-half. And besides me, anoth-er young local boy was making his actual League debut for Derby County – Reg Harrison. Of course, Reg was already an 'old' campaigner, having won an FA Cup medal the previous April. But that season was still one of regional League football, so this was his first game in the Football League too. Before that, Sammy Crooks and Frankie Broome had shared the position.

I would be lying if I said that I wasn't nervous… I certainly was. To play alongside such players as Vic Woodley (England's regular goalkeeper in the years before the war), Jack Howe, Chick Musson, Irish inter-national Peter Doherty, Jack Stamps and Frankie Broome (another pre-war England regular, who moved to centre-forward that day) was something that I had only dared to dream about. Now my long-awaited dream was about to materialise. Unfortunately, the great Raich Carter was injured but it wouldn't be long before he was back in the side and I would play with him too.

In the dressing room all the players immediately put me at ease. Reg Harrison and I were close friends as our wives were both expecting to have our first additions to

Defenders all...in my first League season with Vic Woodley and Jack Howe before the Rams' game at Blackpool in February 1947. We lost 2-1. Raich Carter got our goal.

the family the following year. Reg has one of the most infectious laughs of anyone I have ever met. When he laughs, everybody laughs. There was always a lighthearted attitude in the dressing room and this certainly helped me through that first game. They said that all I had to do was forget the crowd – 28,251 attended that day – and concentrate on the opposition. This I did and although we only made a draw – 2-2 with Peter Doherty scoring them both – at least I hadn't made too many mistakes.

That year we didn't do so well in the League, finishing 14th. However, I had managed to play well enough to be picked for most of the remaining matches and in fact played in exactly half the games in the 42-match programme which went on until 31 May because of the appalling winter.

I also played in all the FA Cup games. As holders, we beat Bournemouth on a waterlogged pitch, then Chelsea in a replay at a frozen Baseball Ground (when Frank Broome had to go in goal after only a few minutes and held out against Tommy Lawton) before losing 1-0 at Anfield in the fifth round.

At the start of the 1947-48 season, I was still in the RAF stationed at Compton Bassett. I remember the late Ben Robshaw writing to the camp commanding officer asking for permission for me to play for the club at weekends. Permission was flatly refused. Luckily I had a friend by the name of Dennis Greenwood who lived in Leeds. Dennis had an MG sports car and the pair of us would sneak out of camp the back way and he would drive me to Derby where I would play and the next day he would pick me up and drive me back to camp. We had managed to get hold of some weekend passes that were not signed by the person who should have signed them. In fact I think we signed one or two of them ourselves!

Looking back, I really don't know how we missed being caught. Had the CO ever looked in the Sunday newspapers on the football page, I would still be in jail!

However, not too long afterwards I had to say goodbye to the many friends I had made, as I was transferred to Huntingdon TTC Command. There it was a totally different story. It was my good fortune to have Group Captain Messenger in command and he was a footballer himself. I approached him to ask for permission to play for Derby County at weekends and instead of the refusal that was given at my last camp, he said to me, "Mozley, if I catch you on camp between Friday and Monday, you are on a charge." Thanks to this man, I was able to make 39 League appearances and play in six FA Cup matches that season.

Big Jack Stamps

IN THE 1947-48 season there was an incident at the Queen's Park Rangers ground, which I will never forget. In order to accommodate as many fans as possible for this sixth-round Cup game, chairs had been placed all the way around the field close to the touchline. When heading a ball, Jack Stamps had received an injury which had resulted in several stitches to his head. Substitutes for injuries were not allowed at this time. He was told to play on the wing and as the ball went out for a throw-in, one of the young 'smart Alecs' sitting on a chair wouldn't give up the ball to Jack. The game was almost over and we were only making a draw 1-1. I'm afraid Jack lost his temper, landed a punch and took the ball away from this guy. It all happened so quickly that no one attempted to do anything and the game went on and ended with a draw. We were to replay on the following Saturday at home.

When we had showered and were ready to board the bus for home, there was a crowd waiting outside that was pretty ugly. Luckily the police were there and we made a hasty retreat to the special bus that accompanied us to the away games.

The following week we beat QPR 5-0. That day, I remember Raich going over to the Queen's Park goalie just before the match started and saying to him, "I'm going to put one goal there (pointing to the left), and another one there (pointing to the right)." Whether this put the man off I don't know – but Raich did exactly that.

Jack Stamps was a strong player – tough as nails – but this was the only time during all the years that I played with him that I ever saw him lose his temper. Many years later, when he'd known for several months that he was going to lose his sight, he also underlined the fact that he was also one of the bravest men that I have ever known.

He never lost his sense of humour and I recall one of the funniest stories that he told me shortly after he had returned from a training centre down in the south of England. At this time he hadn't lost his sight altogether, but in order to simulate what a blind person is going to encounter, they blindfolded Jack and gave him a cane to tap his way along a street. There were, of course, obstacles placed all around the area and each person had to try to get from one end of the street to the other by just using their canes to tap in each direction. Jack said he was doing fine – going up an incline until he suddenly encountered a wall in front of him. So, tapping his way along he turned to his right and found that after two or

Jack Stamps gets up high against QPR in the FA Cup. It was the only time I ever saw Jack lose his temper when he 'chinned' a QPR supporter who wouldn't hand back the ball.

three steps, there was another wall. Changing direction once again he retraced his steps and turned to his left… Two or three steps and there was another wall. He said by this time he was totally confused and the guide who was with him was finding it hard not to laugh. He told Jack he could take off his blindfold and Jack said he almost fell down laughing himself when he did, as he had walked up the incline right into a furniture removal van.

I also recall a match that we played against Bury. It was a Cup game and we were attacking down the right wing. Jack was playing in his usual centre-forward position. Reg crossed a low ball about knee high, right into the six-yard area, and as Jack went to meet it he was just two feet away from a wide open net. The ball hit his knee, rolled up his body and over the top of the goalpost. Jack ended up in the back of the net and the photograph that came out later showed Jack with a wide grin on his face. Jack's Dad was sitting next to my wife in the stands and as all the Bury supporters were clapping and laughing at Jack's big miss, his Dad quipped very dryly, "Well, only our Jack could do that."

Many years later, when I was over from Canada, I contacted Jack, who was living in Burton upon Trent and asked if we could get together. I was staying with my wife's Aunt Etty in the village of Hanbury, which wasn't too far away from Jack's home. We arranged to meet in the local which was the Cock Inn. This was the pub, which was later taken over by Roger Davies. Jack's son,

Our 1947-48 team which lost to Manchester United in the FA Cup semi-final at Hillsborough. Back row (left to right): Stuart McMillan (manager), Tim Ward, self, Leon Leuty, Jock Wallace, Jack Howe, Chick Musson, Jack Poole (trainer). Front row: Reg Harrison, Raich Carter, Jack Stamps, Billy Steel, Angus Morrison.

Ken, drove Nora (Jack's wife) and Jack over to meet Jean, my wife, and me. Jack and Nora had three sons, David, Ken and Peter, and a daughter, Pat. I will tell you a little story about one of them later.

Most of the locals in the pub knew who we were and before long we had a crowd around the table watching Jack and I playing dominoes with his special braille set. Jack played dominoes in the same way that he played football – to win. He knew every move, and as I got down to my last two 'slates', he said to me, "OK Moz, put down your double two and I'm out." Jack knew me for my own sense of humour, so I replied, "OK Stampie, you were looking at my dominoes – I'm not having that!" So Jack said, "Well I thought you didn't see me – you had your head down." The local lads were scratching their heads and looking at each other, as Jack had been blind for some years. We both kept our faces straight and I often wonder what the gossip was about after we had left!

Dolly Townsend – wife of our goalkeeper Billy – and myself judging a beauty contest at an AEU gala at the Municipal Sports Ground, Derby. Dolly killed a blackbird with her first successful attempt at hitting a golf ball!

A little story about Jack's son, Kenneth, still makes my wife Jean laugh when we talk about old times. Most of the wives were very close during those years and visited each other as often as they could. Nora had three boys who were all under the age of five and she lived in

West Green Avenue, close to Whitehurst Street where my wife was living with her parents – I was still in the RAF. On this particular morning, Nora and the boys came over for a cup of tea and as it was a nice day, the boys were playing outside.

My mother-in-law kept a few hens in a pen at the bottom of the garden and all at once there was a squawking and the hens were racing around with the Stamps boys chasing after them! Ken, being inquisitive, had opened the pen and left the gate open. After about half an hour, peace reigned again and the birds were back in their rightful place. They hadn't laid an egg for weeks but the following day, my wife checked and out of the seven hens there were five eggs in the nest boxes. Jean said she would know what to do if they stopped laying again… ask Nora if she could borrow the boys for half an hour!

Nora was one of the most easy going ladies we have ever known. She raised those children and always related the 'catastrophes' that happened with a smile. It was not too long after Christmas and the ladies were having their usual visit when Nora told what happened one morning, not too long after Santa had been. Ken, he was the middle son, had been given a carpenter's set (small hammer, saw etc.) and as it was Sunday morning, Nora and Jack were a bit late in rising. The boys were playing downstairs and were being as good as gold, or so there parents thought. As Nora said later, "We should have known something was going on – they were so quiet!" When they got downstairs, there was Ken, having the time of his life, sawing happily through a leg of a dining room chair. We saw the scars later and in those days I guess they made very realistic toys!

As I am still talking about the wives, there is another story that Jean reminded me of, which happened when the wives decided to go golfing for the day. This was a first time for all of them and I am sure that some very frustrated people, who were golfers, could have cheerfully killed the lot of them. Dolly Townsend, our goalkeeper's wife, decided to hit off first. After four swings, and amidst howls of laughter from the rest of them, she finally connected. However, instead of the ball going down the fairway, it went straight up into a tree and down came not only the ball but also a dead blackbird. I don't know who performed the burial rights but it was the one and only time they ever went golfing. On second thoughts, they were probably barred for life!

Gunners Outgunned

IN 1947, Arsenal were in top form. They were top of the League and had won 17 matches before they were due to play Derby at home on 29 November. I arrived home from the RAF on the Friday and joined the team at the ground. Usually we had a meeting on Friday and discussed with the boss the strategy that he had planned for the game the following day. The previous Saturday, we had beaten Charlton 5-1 and Reg Harrison had got his hat-trick. We all gave Reg his orders: "Just do what you did last week Reg, and 18 will be Arsenal's unlucky number!" Some of you may have been at that match and can still remember the excitement. I know there was a huge crowd – nearly 36,000 – and the roar that went up when Reg scored the winning goal was deafening. Out of the team that played that day, only Reg, Angus Morrison and myself remain. However, it was a great day for the Rams. We stopped the Gunners in their tracks and Reg was the hero of the day.

Jack Howe marks the spot on Lee Leuty's head as I line-up the medicine ball. We were always larking about and on one occasion almost gave trainer Jack Poole a seizure before a big Cup tie.

That same year we gave our trainer Jack Poole a bad time. We were doing well in the Cup rounds and after we had drawn Middlesbrough we were given strict orders not to take any chances and fool around in the gym. We could never see danger and after our usual high spirits in the gym on the Friday before the match, what should happen but Bill Townsend, our goalie, broke his wrist. We managed to weather the storm, though and got through that round safely, 2-1, with a young goalie named Frank Payne. It was the only game he ever played for Derby County's first team – before 43,000 at Ayresome Park. What a baptism of fire!

Jack worried like a mother hen in case any of us got injured again before the next round and looking back it's a wonder we didn't give the poor man an ulcer. After his usual, "now don't do this and don't do that" routine, we

Reg Harrison scores the only goal of the game against Arsenal at the Baseball Ground in November 1947 to end the Gunners' unbeaten run at the start of the season.

couldn't resist the urge to give him another shock. It was decided that I would dust my face down with talc and then pour tomato sauce all over my head and lie in the darkest corner groaning. One of the lads was to go to Jack and tell him that there had been an accident in the gym.

Well, in Jack rushed (sponge in hand) to find me lying in agony and 'bleeding' profusely. He took my wrist – by this time I was 'unconscious' of course – and as he lifted my eyelid I looked up, smiled and said, "Hello Jack". Chick, who could never keep a straight face, was already roaring with laughter and Jack could have killed the lot of us. The standing joke about Jack (who we had nicknamed Cess Poole) was that on one occasion when one of the team was knocked out cold and lying on the field, Jack rushed out with his sponge and attempted to squeeze water over the fallen player's head. Unfortunately he had forgotten to dip the sponge in water beforehand.

Still on the subject of water, at the side of the hot bath was always a cold hose pipe left running and we would try to catch each other with a spray of this when it was least expected. I remember Raich one day getting Lee as he had just stepped out of the bath. Lee jumped right back in and waited for his turn to get his own back. However, Raich managed to get back to the dressing room without a mishap. He came out a little later clad in his undershirt and pretended that he had forgotten all about Lee, who was waiting for his chance to get even. Grabbing the hose, Lee soaked Raich – undershirt and all

– but what he didn't realise was that Raich had gone back to the dressing room and put on Lee's shirt! Thinking that he had scored one over Raich, Lee muttered a few 'unprintables' when he got back to the dressing room and discovered his own dripping shirt hanging on his peg.

In March 1948 I was demobbed from the RAF and began full-time training with the team. My daughter, Lynne, was almost a year old and Derby County rented a house to us in Fairway Close at Allestree. We moved in May and began a friendship with the late Ted Robshaw and his wife Francis that lasted until Ted passed away a few years ago. Ted was the son of Ben Robshaw who was the chairman of Derby County for many years. Ted and his wife, Frances, lived quite close to us, on Kedleston Road. Jean and Frances struck up a friendship when they sat next to each other on the special bus going to the semi-final game at Hillsborough. We would visit each other's homes after the matches and perhaps play cards and as we all had the same sense of humour, we enjoyed each other's company very much. When Ben had to resign from Derby County, Ted joined as a director and was told that his visits to my home had to end as it looked as if he was favouring me over the rest of the team. This, of course, was totally ridiculous but we complied. Ted and Fran didn't come to our house – we went to theirs instead! Jean and Fran still correspond and have been friends now for over 50 years. There is a lot of 'red tape' in every business and Derby County FC proved to be no exception at that time.

Health and Strength

THE house on Fairway Close had a small garage and as I didn't own a car at that time, I decided to get some extra weights and make it into a gym. I didn't lift heavy weights but concentrated on exercises to strengthen my upper body and legs. I had always had an interest in the various body building competitions that were held in England and got to know Wally Wright who was a Derbyshire lad. Wally won the Mr Britain competition and I was asked to present the prizes in London. The following year, I was able to win the Star Gallery Award, given by the *Health and Strength* magazine, for the best physique and thought that finally I was making progress.

At that time, the football club frowned upon weight training and I was asked to stop doing it. As one official put it, "You will get muscle bound." I made my point by saying that I had been building up body strength for the past eight years. I also attributed my speed to the strength in my legs, gained by the exercises that I had done with the weights. They couldn't argue as a report in the newspaper the previous week had said that I was the fastest defender in the League. It wasn't too long after this that Tottenham Hotspur introduced weight training into their team's training programme. I tried unsuccess-fully to get Derby to do the same as I felt that it would be beneficial to everyone, but it was never considered.

The only other team member who became interested in weight training was the big South African, Norman Nielson, who would come for a work-out with me on many occasions. Norman, as some will remember, was an extremely fast defender. He made his debut in the early 1950s and played at centre-half and also centre-forward where his height and strength were a definite advantage.

On several occasions after this, I was called upon to present prizes at the various competitions in London. One year the Mr Universe contest was held there and Jim Park, an American, was the winner. This was before steroids came into the picture and the muscles that these men displayed were earned the hard way. Albert Eccles, from the London area, was another winner with an out-standing body. He also won a Mr Britain competition, and John Lees of Stalybridge was always referred to as 'England's Steve Reeves'. The caption on the *Health and Strength* certificates read, 'Sacred thy body even as thy soul.' In other words: Look after it – you might need it for a long time.

Colin Sheard, who many Derby people will remem-ber, lived until his mid-80s and was a prime example of

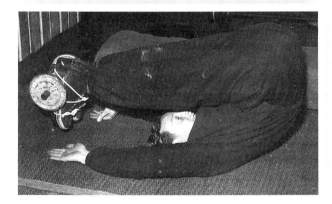

Weight training in the gym which I had created in the garage of our Allestree home at Fairway Close.

this quotation. Colin won the senior Mr Britain contest with a physique that would today be the envy of many 20-year-olds.

During the summer months when the football sea-son was over, we as a team stayed together more than many of the other football teams in the League. We had a pretty good cricket team and helped a lot of the local sides to raise funds by playing on their grounds. We

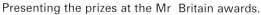
Presenting the prizes at the Mr Britain awards.

looked forward to playing each Sunday, as we were always made so welcome and it was nice for the wives and families as they were always invited too. I remember playing at Melbourne, Belper, Heanor, Burton upon Trent and many of the small villages near Derby.

In a friendly game one Sunday, I remember the best player of the team that we were playing was racking up a good score. I think he just needed a few more runs to beat us, so standing behind the umpire I waited my chance. Jack Parry was bowling and the ball went through and was caught by the wicketkeeper. He made an appeal, but we knew that the batter was safe. So I walked behind the umpire and pushed my arm up under his and gave the out signal. The batter started to walk to the pavilion very dejectedly and it was a long time before the umpire was able to convince anyone that he hadn't called the player out. It all ended in laughter, however, and as usual we all enjoyed our Sunday tea. On another occasion, Frank Broome substituted a large red tomato for a cricket ball and gave a full toss to the opposing batter. He gave a mighty swing and nearly had a fit when it spattered all over the place.

I am convinced that because of the comradeship we had, we were closer as a team than players are today. At one time we had as many as eight local lads playing for Derby. Now it is rare to see

Right: Colin Sheard – Mr Britain winner and a man who many Derby people will remember.

Left: Yours truly after winning the Star Gallery Award given by *Health and Strength* magazine for the best physique.

anything like this as there are so many Europeans playing in the English Leagues. What helped to contribute to our team spirit was the little tea room that was open after the games so that the wives could wait for us inside the building.

Mrs McMillan, the manager's wife, was always on hand. She would make soup for the players at lunchtimes after we had a gruelling workout during our pre-season training sessions and we appreciated all the little things that she would do for us. Once the season was over, we could get together and have a few parties at each other's homes. Chick Musson lived just a few doors away from Frank Broome in Littleover and we have spent many a happy hour at Chick and Ruby's home. Laughter was first and foremost. We would enjoy a beer but I have

Beryl and me with Mr and Mrs Wally Wright. Wally was another Derbyshire lad who won the Mr Britain award.

Presenting more prizes to some champion body-builders.

never seen any of the lads who were in my team at that time the worse for drink.

We had very strict rules to adhere to. It was in your contract that you could not attend a party after Wednesday in any given week during the playing season. No one could enter a public house on the night before a game, not even to deliver tickets. If you were caught doing so it would be an immediate fine and a loss of wages. I can't help wondering what some of the players of today would do if they were confronted with such rules. Especially when our weekly wage was £15 a week if you played in the first team and £12 during the summer season. I still believe, though, that when everyone gets the same wage as we did, there is no jealousy or pettiness. We were a team – we played as a team – and like the old saying goes – we were all for one and one for all.

Always in demand…presenting more prizes, this time at the English Martyrs Catholic Club, Allestree, in 1951.

Enjoying ourselves at a cricket club awards night at Barrow-on-Trent. Jean and me are in the centre of the picture. Jack Stamps and his wife, Nora, are on the right at the back. Jock Wallace, our goalkeeper, is on the left looking away from the camera. And Leon Leuty is seated back left, looking down.

The Rams cricket team of the late 1940s. Back row (left to right): Tim Ward, Jack Stamps, Leon Leuty, Jack Nicholas, Cec Tate, Bert Mozley, Chick Musson and Billy Townsend. Front row: Charlie Ryan, Len Simpson, Raich Carter (who played for Derbyshire), Geoff Knight, Frankie Broome and Rams' assistant secretary, Alex Miller.

Tim Ward and me after batting at Belper Meadows.

Tucking into some of Mrs Stuart McMillan's home-made soup at the Baseball Ground lunch-room. Can you imagine a modern manager's wife getting her apron on and cooking for the players? No, neither can I!

When Broomie's Joke Backfired

FRANK Broome was noted for his humour. He could mimic voices and accents to perfection. I remember one day we were all in the lobby of a hotel and Dougie Taft had recently joined the team. He was in the army at that time doing his two years' National Service, which was mandatory. Doug had been talking about his CO and telling us what a great guy he was and he also mentioned his name. Frank very quietly left and we could see him going over to the 'phone in the lobby. Doug was sitting with his back to Frank, and Frank was motioning to us to keep quiet. Chick, who was always late 'clueing in', was saying, "I wonder what Broomie is up to," while I was kicking him to keep him quiet.

Then a voice came over the loud speaker, "Would Mr Taft of Derby County please accept a call from Captain Thomas." Well Doug jumped up and went red in the face and made a beeline to the desk. We could see him standing to attention and saying, "Yes Sir," and "No Sir," for about five minutes. When he came back, he asked each

Two smartly-dressed young men about town...Frankie Broome and me pictured at a garden party. Frankie had a great sense of humour too.

of us in turn if we had a spare ticket he could have as his CO was coming to the game to watch him. By this time Frank was back and had given us the wink and, of course, none of us could oblige. Poor Doug, who later

I refereed a match involving these Derby solicitors. The goalkeeper is Ken Gregory, who has recently retired from a practice near Derby Cathedral.

kept the Spotted Horse in Derby town centre and then the Osmaston Park Hotel, never did find out that he had had his leg pulled. I think in the end he went to buy a ticket for the non-existent officer.

Another time I remember Frank coming in to tell us all that our opposing team, Blackburn, was staying in the same hotel on the next floor up. If you needed your shoes cleaning, you placed them outside the hotel room at night and then they would be clean for you the next morning. As they were picked up, they were of course

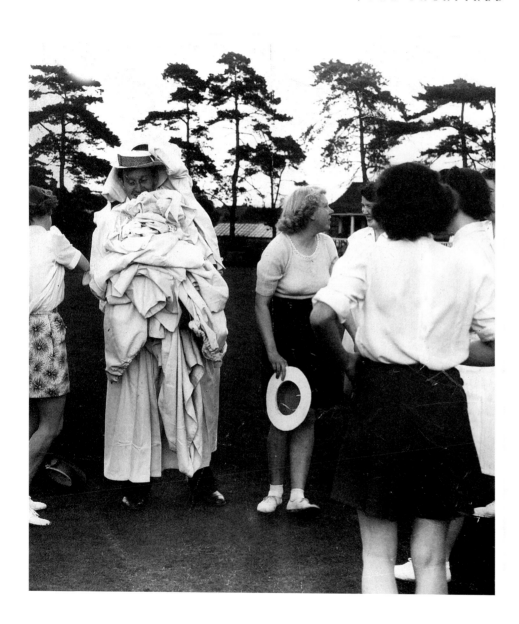

Now I'm weighed down with ladies clothing! I was umpiring a ladies cricket match at Kingsway Hospital.

marked with the room number. It was Christmas time and as was the custom, when playing at Derby, we were not allowed to stay in our own homes. We always stayed at the Midland Hotel. Frank decided he would play the usual 'tie the shoe laces together' trick on the Blackburn players.

After sneaking up to the next floor and collecting about half a dozen pairs, he tied them together and tossed them over the balcony to the floor below. He was laughing about it and saying he would like to see their faces.when they came down to breakfast the next morning without their shoes. However, the joke backfired... Frank had got the wrong floor and the shoes were those of total strangers, who were, to say the least, 'a bit peeved' when their shoes were not returned on time.

Not too long after this, I remember receiving a massage on my leg from Jack Bowers, the old Derby centre-forward and record goalscorer who was now our trainer. He had put some oil on and had the heat lamp overhead while he was loosening up the muscles. All of a sudden the heat lamp exploded and glass flew down on to my legs and hit Jack on his hand. As there was oil on my skin, the glass stuck to it and I was burned quite badly.

We had to laugh later, though, as there was the imprint of Jack's hand quite clearly on my leg with the burns all around it.

Talking of lamps – I remember Dick Cushlow, who was from Chesterfield, complaining one day about some spots that were on his back. We told him to get under the sunray lamp for a few minutes and it would help. Dick did this – but fell asleep and was there for about 15 minutes. When he finally got off the table, his back was as red as a beetroot. He had burned himself and couldn't bear a shirt on for a week. The skin came off his back in strips – but it cured the spots!

England Call-up

IT WAS about this time that I had been getting good reports each week in the newspapers and my name had been mentioned several times as a 'possible' for the right-back position in the England team. I had been chosen to play for the RAF against an FA XI in September 1947 but instead of my usual right-back position, I had been switched to left-back. Our team was fairly strong but could not match the more experienced FA team. Lee Leuty was the centre-half for the FA and played his usual great game. We lost 3-0 but it was after this that I began to get my hopes up that I might be considered for a place on the England team.

My wife had collected the news cuttings of the game and the following reporters had been very kind to me.

News Chronicle: 'Mozley is ready to step into any English side. He showed intelligent positioning and used the ball discreetly.'

Daily Herald: 'If the England selectors learned anything at all, it was that Mozley is just the kind of cool and capable player to take over in the event of injury to George Hardwick.'

Daily Mail: 'Playing on an unaccustomed wing, Mozley outclassed the young Charlton prodigy Lock.

Mozley was the talk among the football managers who thronged the boardroom after the game.'

Anyway, my birthday was coming up, it was mid-September and I waited with growing excitement for the publication of the England team. We had the *Derby Evening Telegraph* delivered and I think both Jean and I were at the front window waiting for the delivery boy to come up the street. On the day that the announcement was due to be made, the paper didn't have time to drop to the floor as we both swooped in and as I looked on the back page… there it was, I had made it! I had my first cap.

A few days later when I received the official card, 'England v FA of Ireland', it read: 'All players will be allowed travelling expenses and a fee of £20.' Underneath that it also mentioned that we must take our own soap and towels! I wonder if they still do?

That day in Liverpool was a disaster for me. We played at Goodison Park and the team included Johnny Morris of Manchester United and Jesse Pye, who was playing for Wolves at that time. Both men would eventually sign for Derby County, of course.

Ireland played above themselves and for our part we missed goal after goal. I recall the ball was passed to

Peter Desmond and I made a sliding tackle. I got to the ball but also fetched Desmond down. The referee immediately pointed to the penalty spot. I felt devastated. My first international and I had given away a penalty. I felt sure that was the beginning and end for me with the England team. We lost that game – the first time England had ever been beaten at home by a non-UK country – and the newspapers the following day berated the team for such a poor showing. However, I was surprised to read that I wasn't blamed for the penalty and was considered to have played reasonably well in my first international. This didn't help much as I was convinced that I had wrecked my chances of getting picked a second time.

However, a few weeks later, I was again selected to play against Wales and this time we won comfortably and I had a good game. Blackpool's

The proud owner of an England cap – my first, won against the Republic of Ireland, although the outcome was an unhappy one. I gave away a penalty and we lost.

England training with (from left to right) Johnny Morris, Tom Finney and Neil Franklin.

Stan Mortensen replaced Johnny Morris while Jesse lost his place to Jackie Milburn of Newcastle. In October, I was selected to play against Northern Ireland and earned my third cap. The next international game was to be against Italy and I was delighted to get news that I had been chosen again. However, that was to be the end of

I'm shaking hands with Leon Leuty after we were both selected to play for the Football League.

my international appearances as the Saturday before the game. I pulled a muscle. I had to inform the England manager that I was unfit to play and although I was sent two free tickets to go and see the game, it was with a heavy heart that I watched Alf Ramsay playing in my number-two shirt. I was never picked again until 1950 when I went on the Canadian tour with a representative England team.

Talking of Johnny Morris reminded me of the time he was sent off the field. We were playing Portsmouth at

Special training? Johnny Morris, self, Leon Leuty, Jack Stamps and Tim Ward playing goal at Kedleston.

I'm in action against Spurs at the Baseball Ground in October 1952 and, according to Press reports, had an outstanding game in front of the chairman of the England selectors. But an international recall never came in what was our relegation season.

home and Jimmy Scoular, who was known for rough play, had fouled Johnny. Something was said and before you knew it – John had connected with a blow to Scoular's 'bread basket'. He went down like a sack of potatoes. Johnny knew he would be sent off and as I went

over to him he quipped, "Bert, is anybody watching?" I said, "Well John, just a few thousand." "Alright," he said, "pretend to help me and I'll limp off." I had to laugh at the time because it was so typical of the humour that existed throughout the team. Johnny was suspended for two weeks without pay, and as he had a family to support, we all 'chipped in' and made up his wages.

Christmas 1949 was a time that I shall never forget. Unless it was from a penalty kick, it was unusual for a full-back to score. It was the day after Boxing Day and we were playing Birmingham at home. Gil Merrick, the England goalkeeper, was in great form as usual. Derby were given a free-kick and I lobbed a shot over to the far post from well back of the halfway line. I don't remember if there was a wind that day but Gil misjudged its flight and it went in the top corner of the net over his head. It was just a lucky shot but I kidded Gil after the game, saying, "You never saw that one Gil did you? I placed it just where I wanted it." I only scored two goals during my career with Derby. The other goal was against Manchester United, also close to Christmas, the year before… but I have to confess, I don't recall doing it at all.

"I'll Hang You on That Clothes Peg!"

SINCE joining the club and playing in the first team, my regular partner at left-back was Jack Howe. Jack was a good friend to me when I first started playing with the team. He helped me a lot and was never critical when I made a mistake. I remember the afternoon that Billy Steel made himself very unpopular. We were playing Liverpool at home on a frozen pitch and as I raced down the wing to cut Billy Liddell off, I beat him to the ball but it bounced on a piece of frozen turf and Billy was able to take the ball towards the goal. He took a shot but luckily it was well wide.

At half-time, Billy Steel came over to me and said, "Mozley – it's your job to clear the ball – leave that fancy stuff to me." He was serious. Well, Jack Howe heard him say this and he went over to have a few choice words with him. I guess Billy said something that Jack didn't like and Jack was heard to say, "Any more of this and I'll hang you on that clothes peg Steel." Jack had the strength to do it too. Incidentally, he was the only player in the League at that time to wear contact lenses. Many's the time that we all had to go crawling in the gym on our hands and knees because Jack had lost a lens…

Chick Musson, Leon Leuty and Tim Ward were the half-backs in front of us, resulting in a solid defence. Not only was Tim a good right-half, he was also a great cricketer. Like Lee Leuty, who played at the same time as the great centre-half Neil Franklin, Tim was unfortunate to be around at the same time as Willie Watson of Sunderland, coincidentally also a fine cricketer, good enough to play the first-class game in fact. Tim was deserving of England recognition on many occasions. I know that I was glad to have him in front of me for all those years that we were at Derby together.

We had several goalkeepers but Billy Townsend was the most regular choice. Billy always had a bit of a weight problem and was nicknamed Billy Bunter. In the off season he would gain about ten pounds. When we started training for the new season, he would put on a rubber jacket and jog for miles. He was a very dedicated man and was always able to take off the excess weight

The Rams in 1948-49. Back row (left to right): Jack Poole (trainer), Tim Ward, self, Terry Webster, Leon Leuty, Chick Musson, Jack Howe. Front: Reg Harrison, Johnny Morris, Jack Stamps, Billy Steel, Frankie Broome.

before the new season began. One of the funniest incidents that I remember about Billy was the day that we played at the Baseball Ground and the fog rolled in. It was a real 'pea-souper' and you could barely see the halfway line from the goals. As the afternoon wore on it got worse and in the end the referee had to call the players off in the hope that visibility would improve. We all straggled back into the dressing room one by one. We had been there for quite some time when somebody said, "Hey, where's Billy?" No one had thought to tell him and he was still out there in goals, peering in vain through the fog. That was the only time in my career that I remember a game that was delayed because of fog. It was also a bad day for me as well because when play was resumed – I pulled a muscle.

There was also a time when we played at Liverpool and Billy was getting 'razzed' by the crowd behind the goal. As he turned round to look at them, I was heading back towards the goal to take a goal kick. Suddenly, an orange came sailing through the air straight for Bill. I ran forward and managed to catch it, thanking the crowd and pretending to peel it. I guess we were winning at the time as I got a few angry boos from the Liverpool crowd. Fortunately nothing else was thrown our way. Back then the supporters were pretty well behaved. Some of the fiascoes that take place these days between opposing fans make me wonder where and how it all started. There was the odd scrap, of course, but never the riots that took place during some of the games in more recent times.

That first week back in training after the summer season was hard on the system. If you needed to break in a new pair of football boots you ordered a pair that was a size too small. You would have to grease your feet to get into the boots, which were of course leather, and then sit with your boots on and your feet in a bathtub of hot water. Then when the water had totally soaked into the leather, you walked until they were moulded to the shape of your foot. After that it was just like wearing a pair of slippers as they fit perfectly. Unfortunately I always lost the nails on my two big toes each time I had to break in a new pair of boots.

In October 1949, Jack Howe played his last game for Derby and went to Huddersfield and later to King's Lynn where he took over a pub. It ended our three-year partnership and I was sorry to see my old pal go. Jack Parr was brought from the reserve team and played well enough to hold his place for two years until Geoff Barrowcliffe took over in 1951. Geoff stayed and kept his place until long after I had left the club in 1955. He was a strong player and played both the right and left-back positions equally well during his long career with Derby.

We used to wonder if he carried his own rabbit's foot with him everywhere he went. He was the luckiest man I have ever met when it came to gambling. On the train going down to play one of the London teams, we would get a game of poker going, It didn't matter what Geoff picked up – he was a winner. If he bet on a horse – it came first. It seemed as if everything he touched turned to money when we played cards. Well, one day, we had another journey by train to Blackpool and as usual, on the way there, we played cards and Geoff once again, was the winner.

While in Blackpool, I walked around the shops and found this place that sold trick cards. Buying a pack without being noticed proved a bit difficult but I managed to hide what I was doing and told the lads who were waiting for me that I had picked up something for my daughter. In the hotel room that night I was able to read the instructions for the backs of the cards and was able to tell at a glance both the suits and the numbers. It didn't take me long to get pretty good at knowing how to add up to 21. I don't recall the score at Blackpool that day but I do remember the fun I had going home on the train. I casually opened the deck and we sat down to play. This time I suggested we play Pontoon, as I knew I could read the backs of the cards easier playing that game. I didn't lose a hand all the way back to Derby and the team couldn't figure out why I had suddenly become so lucky. As the train drew into the Derby station, they were reckoning up what they had lost and I couldn't keep a straight face any longer. They all got their money back, of course, but they wouldn't let me play with my cards again.

We were always playing tricks on each other and I remember when we went on what was called 'special

The Rams in 1949-50. Back row (left to right): Tim Ward, self, Bert Mozley, Billy Townsend, Jack Parr, Ken Oliver, Chick Musson. Front: Les Mynard, Johnny Morris, Jack Stamps, Billy Steel, Hughie McClaren. By now, Lee Leuty and Jack Howe had moved on, unsettled by the presence of Billy Steel.

training' to Mappleton, a small village close to Ashbourne. This would be the week before the FA Cup matches were due to begin. The idea was so that we wouldn't be pestered morning, noon and night by friends wanting Cup tickets. We would come back to Derby each morning to train and then return to this large guesthouse, which was taken over by the club. It was an old-style country house with landings and rooms leading off in different directions.

One of the favourite tricks was to wait until someone had left their room and then go and upset their bed and tie up all the sheets. If their suitcase was handy, so much the better. The contents of that would be taken out and hidden in different places. On this particular night, we decided to pick on Jack Howe. Jimmy McGill went inside his room to strip the bed and I kept watch outside the door. Unfortunately for us, Jack came back sooner than expected and I wasn't able to warn Jimmy in time to get him out. It was a big old-fashioned bedroom, with a large wardrobe against the wall so Jimmy, being quite small, nipped inside the wardrobe. Jack went into his room, did a bit of swearing and straightened up his bed.

He came out on to the landing, brought a chair with him to sit on and said, "Well that's the last time anybody upsets my bed. I'm staying right here." Jimmy, hearing this, came out of the wardrobe and stripped the bed again. In the meantime, Chick Musson had gone scouting around the grounds and found a ladder. He propped it up against the bedroom window and Jimmy made a hasty retreat. You can imagine the yell that went up from Jack's room when he went in and found his bed tipped upside down again. If anyone had come into the guest house at that time, they would have thought we were all crazy. Each team member was walking around with a suitcase in his hand, not daring to leave it behind in the room. It was just like a scene out of one of the old Marx Brothers movies.

"Have You Got Any Spare Bacon?"

FOOD rationing was still a part of life in England, right up until the early 1950s. Although the war was over, it took a long time to get stocked up with enough food so that the ration books could be thrown away. I remember one day when just a few of us had stayed indoors at Mappleton, a man came into the guesthouse and asked us if we had any spare Cup tickets. I believe it was Frank Broome who looked at him and said, "Yes. Have you any spare bacon?" Well, the man reeled off everything he had in his grocer's shop – and we told him that we would do an exchange deal. He took us to his shop in Ashbourne and we loaded up with groceries.

There was Reg, Chick, Frank and myself and we couldn't carry the boxes as they were so heavy. He had given us butter, sugar, bacon, all the luxuries that we couldn't get and the special bus that brought us back to the Baseball Ground also took us to our individual homes to unload the groceries. When I carried everything in the house, my mother-in-law had a fit. If you

I'm nicely balanced in a tackle against Harold Bodle during a fourth-round FA Cup tie against Bury in January 1950.

were caught with what was called 'black-market' items, it was an offence and you were heavily fined. I can

The team which lost 2-1 to Manchester United at Old Trafford in October 1951. Back row (left to right): Ken Oliver, self, Ray Middleton, Geoff Barrowcliffe, Colin Bell, Steve McLachlan. Front: Reg Harrison, Johnny Morris, Jack Stamps, Jack Parry, Hughie McClaren. Steve McLachlan was the 'eternal reserve' at the Baseball Ground. He joined the Rams in 1938 and remained until 1953 but made less then 60 appearances during that time.

I'm the one with the pipe, watching Ken Oliver try a snooker shot at the Baseball Ground. Other from left to right are Colin Bell, Hughie McClaren, Geoff Barrowcliffe, Jack Parry, Steve McLachlan and Reg Harrison.

All together at the Baseball Ground. Back row (left to right): Ken Oliver, Geoff Barrowcliffe, Ray Middleton, self, Norman Neilson. Front: Jack Stamps, Reg Harrison, Hughie McClaren, Stuart McMillan (manager), Steve McLachlan and Colin Bell.

remember her hiding the sugar away up in the bathroom. I think the butter went in a box in the pantry, (no fridges in those days) and the bacon and tea were put underneath the bathtub. She was a very nervous person at the best of times and you can imagine what a state she was in when she came to our bedroom to awaken us late that night with the words, "Oh dear Bert, there's a policeman at the door. Whatever shall we do." I opened the bedroom window to look outside and a voice said, "Bert, have you got a Cup ticket to spare? I've got a load of lard here if you want to swap. My uncle owns a fish and chip shop and he has some left over." His name was Les Oliver – and Les, if you are still around, I want you to know how much you scared my mother-in-law that night. I guess the same thing happened at Reg Harrison's house where Wyn had him climbing up into the attic to hide everything too.

Another year at Mappleton when we were special training, a man by the name of Sammy Ramsden came over to the guest house. Sam owned the local dance hall in Derby called the Plaza Ballroom. Petrol was also rationed and no one was allowed to use a private car to travel where a bus route was available. We asked Sam how he had got there and he said he had driven his car. He laughed and said he could always get some petrol. Keeping my face straight I said, "Is that right Sam? I shall have to let my Uncle Horatio know about this." (Of course Chick was already laughing but luckily Sammy didn't notice.) "Well," said Sammy, "who is your uncle?" "Do you know Chief Constable Rawlings?" I replied.

"Well – er – yes er," Sam stuttered, "Now Bert, would you like some silk stockings for your wife?" and Sammy produced these packets from his case and started to hand them around. I guess that in the end he got his tickets as silk stockings were also a luxury item and I think I earned a few 'Brownie' points that day when I presented them to my wife. We made Sam sweat a little though, in spite of the fact that Chick as usual, nearly gave the show away by laughing at the wrong time.

They Say The Good Die Young

CHICK Musson was one of the most likeable men in the team. He didn't have a mean bone in his body. He was a team man through and through. He tackled hard but was never deliberately dirty. When I see some of the antics that take place on the field today with the dives and pretence of injuries, I think of Chick. We were playing in Holland, having been invited to tour, and during one of the games, Chick went forward into a tackle but the studs on his boots were too long. They jammed into the ground and he went over on his ankle. He was in severe pain but carried on until the end of the match when his boot had to be cut off. He had fractured his ankle. Although he tried to come back after this, he was never quite the same and eventually lost his place in the team. It was a great shock to everyone when Chick died at such an early age.

Leon Leuty, too, died very soon after Chick and it was with a heavy heart that I read of the passing of them

With Lee Leuty in Germany.

The irrepressible Chick Musson. He was never the same player after being injured during our match in Holland.

both. Lee was one of the coolest centre-halves I have ever known. It was unfortunate that he was around at the same time as Neil Franklin and Billy Wright as I feel sure that otherwise, he would have commanded a place in the England team. Many people claimed that Lee was an even better player than Wright and I would second that without hesitation.

I smile recalling the time Derby County went to Germany. We were the first football team to play over in Europe after the war and played against a select Army XI. Our transportation started at the airport at Burnaston and we all piled into two Lancaster bombers. Inside there were no seats and we sat down on the floor on each side of the plane. One of the aircrew asked if anyone would like to go to the rear and sit in the gunner's section; this was a plexi-glassed small area on a swivel at the back of the 'plane and it took Lee about five minutes to climb inside and sit down. We were approaching Holland and the two 'planes were flying fairly close to each other. Our pilot asked if we would like to see the flooding of Holland and as he made a descent, the pilot of the other 'plane had decided to do the same thing. All of a sudden from going down – we were all landing in a heap on top of each other, as the 'plane had gone into what seemed to be an almost vertical climb. It had taken Lee five minutes to get into the rear gunner's compartment but in five seconds he was out and asking, "What the **** happened?" We learned afterwards what a narrow escape we all had. Our 'plane

The Rams party pictured in Germany in August 1945, after a scary journey by Lancaster bomber.

almost touched the other one before our pilot made the upward climb. I think the old Lancasters all had Rolls-Royce engines… I was glad they didn't fail us on that day! I wasn't the only Ram to kiss the ground when we got off the 'plane in Germany. We all did! Lee's complexion was a very nice shade of pale green for quite some time and we pulled his leg about being a rear gunner on many occasions after that.

After Lee had left the club his place was taken by Ken Oliver, who came from Sunderland. Ken was another great personality. I have never seen anyone head a ball quite like he did. He was nicknamed 'rubber-neck' with good reason. Ken was a good club man and stayed in the first team for seven years. He never put on weight and yet he could eat more than all the team put together! I don't know how his wife Sadie managed to stay out of the kitchen. I had a good appetite – but Ken could beat me when it came to eating. He was usually first to start his meal and the last to finish wherever we went.

It was around this time that Albert Mays also joined the first team. There is quite a funny story I recall that involved Hughie McClaren (who was our left winger), Albert and myself. Hughie had an Alsatian dog that had given birth to puppies. As he couldn't keep them he was going to have to put them to sleep. Well Jean, my wife, is and always has been a dog lover. We had two small children at that time but she couldn't bear the thought of healthy puppies being killed. In a weak moment we agreed to take one of the pups and Albert's wife said she

would take the other. We called our dog Timmy and in the space of three months he grew into the biggest dog we have ever owned.

I had built a brand new fence in the back garden so that he would have some space to play and one Sunday afternoon the fence was finished and Timmy was let outside without me having to tie him up. He loved his freedom and was happily playing with a ball so we went inside for lunch. Just after lunch as we sat in the front room looking out on to the fields that bordered Allestree Lane, Jean said, "Look at that dog chasing that poor horse out there." The horse was kicking up his heels and was narrowly missing the dog. We were really angry with the owners who obviously didn't care where their dog was. We watched for a few minutes and I said, "It looks like a dog similar to our Tim doesn't it." Jean, taking a second look said, "I think it IS our Tim." Rushing to the back garden – there was my fence lying in shreds on the floor. Tim had got fed up with his ball and decided that the green pastures with a horse included looked a lot more fun. So much for my carpentry work… and it took me an hour to get him back. The following day I asked my Dad if he would come and give me a hand with the fence. Every man to his trade!

In the meantime, Albert's wife, Beryl, hadn't had much luck with their dog either. He had also grown to a gigantic size and when he didn't want to obey a command he would bare his teeth and 'smile' at her. This particular day, he had also been playing out in the garden and with muddy paws had raced inside, up the stairs and leaped on to their bed which had a beautiful white satin eiderdown and bedspread covering it. Beryl said she tried everything to get him off, all to no avail, and every time she went near him the growl and smile changed her mind. She had to wait until Albert came home before he would get down. I don't think the bedspread ever looked the same again. Albert Mays, by the way, was a brilliant snooker player and was one of the best cricketers that we had. He also died at a very early age as did Hughie, Lee and Chick.

As Al Read used to say, take it on the chin with a grin! With Ken Oliver and one of the winners of a fancy dress parade. Ken took over from Lee when he left the Rams.

Canada the Beautiful

IN MAY 1950, I had the good fortune to accompany a strong FA party on a six-week tour of Canada. Little did I know that this was to change my life. We sailed on the *Empress of Scotland* on 15 May from Southampton. The boat had been a troopship during the war but had been re-fitted for the cruise line and this was its first voyage after the re-fit. Our team included many of the top stars of the day including the 'Wizard of dribble himself' Stanley Matthews. Stan had used the bathroom in his cabin and then left to join the team up on deck. We would pass the time heading or tapping the football to each other as we stood in a circle on the deck. During this time we lost about six footballs over the side and I often wondered afterwards, what happened to them… if they had washed up on some far away shore. Anyway, after we had finished our training session, we all returned to the cabins and when Stan entered his, he

With Jimmy Hagan, who used to play for the Rams before the war, on the FA's Canadian tour in 1950, pictured in Stanley Park, Vancouver.

This time I'm lining up with (from left to right) Rams colleague Tim Ward, Nat Lofthouse and Jackie Sewell.

was up to his ankles in water. A pipe had not been connected properly after the re-fit and not only was Stan's cabin flooded but six more cabins too! Luckily the cruise was not fully booked and a quick change ensued. We teased Stan and accused him of trying to sink the ship before we had even started off on the tour.

At dinner that night, we all enjoyed a great meal and retired early as it was to be training as usual while on board. We set sail at high tide and all reported for breakfast. At lunchtime there were five missing… I was one of the five. At dinner that night – another three were missing and the following day I understand that only about five showed up for breakfast. We were all seasick for two or three days but eventually gained our 'sea-legs'.

We landed at Montreal and were taken to the Chateau Frontenaque, which was the hotel where we were to spend the next few days. At that time, Canada did not have a very strong representative side. Soccer, as it was called, had not caught on and was just played at the amateur level. Football was the term they used for a type of rugby played in North America. Ice hockey – or just 'hockey' to them – of course was their national game. It is understandable why our type of football was slow gaining popularity. For one thing, the climate in most of the provinces wouldn't permit the game to be played during the winter months. Temperatures of 40

Stan Milburn and me in the USA.

degrees below zero were common, with perhaps the exception being British Columbia. When you consider that the difference between Vancouver and Montreal is a matter of over 3,000 miles, then, of course, travelling could be a major factor too.

We played in Montreal on 20 May and managed to beat them comfortably 7-0. In Toronto the opposition was a little tougher and the score was 4-1. Our next stop was in Saskatoon, Saskatchewan, and as it was just a small town with virtually no soccer teams to chose from

The FA party photographed at Niagara Falls.

we ran up a score of 19-1. On to Vancouver after by train which was a day and a half ride away and there we met stronger opposition. We made a draw 4-4 but the pitch we played on was more or less gravel. Then came the ferry ride to Victoria which is the capital city of British Columbia.

Without question Victoria is one of the most beautiful cities in the world. The ferry pulled into the harbour and we crossed the street and entered the Empress Hotel. This was an élite, very expensive and yet old fashioned hotel. Home to the wealthy old ladies who were all sitting very sedately in the lounge as we walked in. I can't say that we were the quietest of teams and the man on the desk made a fatal mistake when he asked one of the lads to refrain from whistling inside the 'hallowed halls'. After that – one or two always made a point of doing just that as they walked past him at the desk.

Jimmy Hancocks from Wolves was usually missing from the rest of the team on the boat and we would find him playing bingo with all the old ladies. It was the same at the hotel. There was Jimmy sitting very comfortably with them in the lounge drinking tea and chatting as if he had known them for years! We stayed just two days in Victoria and then returned to play a combined British Columbia team in Vancouver. It was there that whilst we were playing on the field, someone broke into the dressing room and took all the money out of the wallets. Luckily I had spent most of mine on gifts but some of the lads lost quite a lot of dollars. The next call was in Calgary, Alberta, and this was something quite special on the tour.

The journey through the Rockies from Vancouver to Calgary is spectacular. Songs have been written about the blue Canadian Rockies and yes – those mountains really do look blue. Our arrival in the 'cow town' as it is called was one of the most memorable. We were each presented with a white Stetson, which is symbolic of the town. There we met a man named Arthur Davis who was the president of the Calgary Soccer Association. His father, George, who we had met in Vancouver two days before, was from Alfreton. He played for the Rams in 1903 and was capped at that time. His photograph wearing the England shirt and cap was next to my own in the boardroom.

We arrived at lunchtime and after checking in at the hotel, we were asked by Mr Davis what we would like to do. We were given the choice of going horseback riding or golfing. As I had slightly pulled a muscle in Vancouver, I decided to go riding, having visions of a slow amble through the countryside. That was my first mistake. My total experience of horses to that date was a sixpenny ride on the donkeys up and down Blackpool beach but I wasn't going to tell anybody that. Together with Nat Lofthouse of Bolton, Reg Flewin from Portsmouth and Frank Bowyer from Stoke, we left for the stables with Mr Davis's wife, Margaret. The horses were saddled up and ready to go. The lady owner of the ranch asked who was the best rider. Not one of us had ridden before but Reg Flewin, getting his own back on me as I had pulled his leg a time or two on the journey, pointed to me and said, "He is." I wasn't going to say "No, I wasn't," in front of both the ladies so her next words were, "Well, I'll give you the black horse over there." I eyed the horse and he looked quite calm so I began to breathe a little easier and managed a smile.

However, it was soon wiped off my face when she added, "Unfortunately he threw my husband a year ago and he broke his neck, but if you keep a tight rein on him you'll be fine." Well, I caught the slight grins on the faces of the other lads and didn't quite know how I could get out of it at that point. Deciding that as I was in this far I might as well carry it through, I hopped up into the saddle with the best imitation of Roy Rogers that I could muster. I had my camera slung around my neck and with Mrs D in the lead, off we went over the foothills. Looking back – we must have looked a right motley crew. We were all wearing our grey flannels and black England jackets – not at all suitable for riding. After walking along through a field we came to some flat ground and Mrs Davis decided to put her horse into a canter.

The rest of us followed but to my dismay, my horse was what they called a trotter. I was bouncing up and down in the saddle and my camera kept coming up and hitting me under the chin and I was holding on with my knees for all I was worth! We had just booked the horses for an hour but it was the longest hour of my life…

The next day, none of us could walk straight. We had a good laugh about it later but we were all chaffed and sore for three days. Luckily we weren't booked to play until 10 June in Winnipeg, Manitoba.

When we arrived in Winnipeg, the town was just recovering from one of the worst floods in its history. We could see in the downtown area where the water had left its mark on the buildings. We played an exhibition game and then left for Toronto to play against Manchester United who was also on a tour of Canada. A private group of businessmen, who said they would make sure we would be looked after financially, promoted this game. They had sold about 15,000 tickets. We were looked after alright! We were each presented with a very cheap looking cigarette lighter after the match… None of us smoked! We had a good game against Manchester that day, though, and won 4-2.

Two days later, we paid a visit to New York. What a city! We were given the royal treatment and wined and dined at the Waldorf Astoria Hotel. We were driven by bus around the city and our driver pointed out all the sights. We were also driven through Harlem and were told then by the driver that you never drive your car there unless you have all the doors locked first. Looking out on to the streets at some of the men who were standing around on each street corner, I was glad that we didn't run out of petrol. I think all the lads on the bus breathed a sigh of relief when we finally drove out of the area.

An FA XI on the Canadian tour. I'm second from left on the back row. Blackpool's Harry Johnston is on my left and Derby's Tim Ward is at the end of the row. Stan Matthews is extreme right on the front row. Nat Lofthouse is centre and next to him is Jimmy Hagan.

The USA hadn't been taking football very seriously up until that year. They had a national team and had brought coaches in from Europe. As was (and still is) their custom, they didn't spare the dollars and formed quite a good team to play against us. It was a close game and we managed to win 1-0 with a goal scored by Johnny Hancocks. Just a week or so later, this same team beat the England team 1-0 in the World Cup in Brazil. We were on our way home by boat when news of England's defeat came through. Our ship's captain, who was a football enthusiast, flew the flag at half-mast until we arrived home.

I felt really sorry for him though a little later. As our boat sailed into Southampton, the captain came down and agreed to have his photograph taken with some of the top ice skaters of the day who had travelled back from competing in North America. They grouped together and the captain removed his hat and placed it under his arm. He was totally bald. Just as the photographer had them all set, a seagull flew overhead and 'splat' – a bullseye – right on top of the captain's head. With all the England team watching, a roar of laughter went up and I feel sure that the poor man wished he could be

Aboard that darned horse! I'm about to be taken on the journey of a lifetime.

anywhere but on deck at that time.

We had returned to Montreal after the game in New York, to play our last game, against a Swedish team who was also touring Canada. The team was Jonkopping and we were able to beat them 7-1. I was not playing on this particular day and a Mr Davies, who was one of the England team officials, asked me to keep an eye on the door of the dressing room when the team was changing and keep out any one who was trying to interview the team. He had noticed that some members of the press had been smoking in the changing rooms and did not think this was good for the players.

As the lads were all sitting around waiting for the game to start, there was a knock on the door. I asked who was there and the voice replied, "It's Mr Davies." There was a doorman in uniform also with us so I asked him to loan me his peaked cap and coat. I opened the door a little and with the cap over my eyes said, "I'm sorry but no one is allowed inside." I shut the door and by this time all the team was laughing. This happened about four times and each time Mr Davies was getting more and more desperate, trying to tell me that he was an official with the team. I kept opening the door and then closing it again, repeating that I was sorry but Mr Davies had left orders that no one is allowed to enter. In the end, I thought I'd better let him in before he blew his top. Upon seeing me standing there, and all the team laughing, he just rolled his eyes and said he might have known it would be me.

He was a really good sport as I had previously pulled another trick on him when we were crossing the border from Canada to play in New York. I had noticed his passport lying on a table so picked it up and put it in my pocket. When we got to the border we were, of course, asked for our identification. We all showed our passports and I could see Mr Davies frantically searching pockets and cases and looking a very worried man. It was at that point when they were refusing to let him into the country that I magically 'found' his passport. He took it all in good part, though, and was a very understanding and patient man. We had a lot of fun on that tour and I know I made some lifetime friends.

A New Beginning

ONE of the men that I met in Canada came on holiday to England in 1953. He and a friend had called at the Detroit plant in the USA and bought a brand new Cadillac car to drive around England and France. I remember we were playing at Blackpool and as I led the team out of the tunnel this man leaned over the side and shouted to me. I knew the face but couldn't think where I had met him. After the match, it suddenly came to me. It was the man from Calgary, in Alberta, whose wife had taken us riding that day. He was waiting for me outside the Blackpool ground and we had a chat and arranged to meet in Derby the next day.

We had two daughters by that time, Lynne and Lea, so couldn't accommodate Art and Gus, his friend, as we didn't have the space. However, Jean made them welcome and they came to dinner several times and took us out in the Cadillac. It was so wide that we couldn't drive it into our driveway so had to leave it on the street. I was having fits in case it was damaged but Art didn't seem to mind at all. I learned at this time that he was the owner of several large hotels in Calgary and that football was a game he enjoyed watching. While he was in Derby, he had a 'phone call from home to say that his mother was very ill and not expected to live. He immediately decided to cut his holiday short and fly back. As his friend Gus was a lot older than Art, he didn't want to drive this car in England. It was arranged that I would drive it back to Liverpool and put it on the boat for them on the due date, which was around the middle of June, after our season ended. He gave me some money for petrol and said I could use the car as often as I wished.

The first day I drove it to the ground all the directors, staff and players, came out to have a look at it. Much to my relief, the directors gave me permission to leave it in their car park. I still have to laugh at one wag who came up to me and said, "Hey Bert, did you get your benefit?" My benefit would have just about bought a pair of wheels on that Cadillac but I just laughed at him and said, "No, I won it in a raffle." For a few weeks, I felt like a millionaire but was glad when I finally drove to Liverpool without a mishap and met Gus. Handing over the car to him, he just had to drive it on to the boat and that was the end of my association with Cadillacs.

At this time I was captain of the club and one of my duties was to tell the rest of the team to stay behind after

The happiest day of our lives – Lea comes home from hospital.

training when the boss wanted to talk to them. Once or twice, I had pulled their legs and told them to wait while keeping my face straight. Well, of course they would sit there patiently, I would go home and it would be a while before they caught on that I had been kidding them.

This particular Friday, Stuart McMillan had said, "Bert, I want to have a short meeting before we play Charlton tomorrow. I'll meet you all after training." I remember going into the gym and saying, "OK lads – we have a meeting today, Stu wants to talk about the game tomorrow." For some reason I was the last to have my

Those wonderful Sheffield nurses. Here, one of those lovely girls holds Lea. This period in our life was also one which fostered transfer rumours!

shower and as I made my way to the room where we were to have our meeting, I thought it was a bit quiet. When I got there – there wasn't a soul in sight. They all thought I was pulling their leg again and had gone home. My humour had really backfired on me that time and I got a dressing down from Stu when he learned what had happened. Luckily we beat Charlton the next day.

Actually, Charlton was the one London team that we were always lucky against. We could almost guarantee a win. Against Stoke, it was just the reverse. They were my bogey team. I never seemed to play well at Stoke and remember feeling depressed the minute we drove into the town.

It was unfortunate that by this time quite a lot of dissension was apparent in the team. It had started with the arrival of Billy Steel. He was given so many 'extras' which the rest of the team didn't get, that several players decided they wanted transfers. In those days we had no agents and would receive only ten per cent of any transfer fee. Very few players were in what you could call the 'wealthy' bracket. You played because you loved the game and the honour that came from playing for your local team. We had lost several key players and although we still had some good forwards, the team spirit just wasn't there. That year Billy Steel left the club and Jack Lee came and took over the centre-forward spot with Jack Stamps and Johnny Morris as his inside-forwards.

At this point, I have to mention a player who in my

I'm Father Christmas at the Rams players' Christmas party. Our daughter Lynne wasn't fooled. She recognised Daddy's nose!

opinion was one of the most under-rated forwards ever to play for Derby County. I refer to Tommy Powell. Tom could play in any position on the forward line and had one of the best body swerves in the League. He could also bring down a ball just as if it was fastened to the toe of his boot. I have never seen anyone else do it in quite the way that he could. He was another player who was definitely capable of playing for England but was unlucky to have been overlooked.

For 20 years, Tom, a Derby lad, was a one-club man. Nowadays, a team is lucky to hold on to a player for 20 weeks before they are asking for a transfer. A player such as Tommy Powell is one of a very rare breed these days. I was very sad to hear of his sudden death in the autumn of 1998. Typically, he had just been to address a meeting of disabled Rams fans, along with another dear pal of mine, Reg Harrison.

Once the team started to break up, it didn't take long for the Rams to slide quickly down the League table. In the 1950-51 season we finished in 11th position. The following year, we finished in 17th place and the year after that, 1952-53, was the saddest year of all for me as we were relegated to the Second Division. Johnny Morris was transferred and although several newcomers from the reserve team were given try-outs, somehow the old magic had left the team. That year we scored only 59 goals and without scoring power the writing was on the wall. Things went from bad to worse and the following year we were relegated to the Third Division. This was May 1954.

The season had just ended and I had word from Canada that George Davis, who was Art's father, was coming over to England on holiday. He was, if you remember, the old Derby player and international, who came from the Alfreton district and through George I was later to meet a lot of very nice people from that area. He had lost his wife and was coming to visit his sister-in-law in Nottingham. This time, the car he brought with him was a Lincoln Continental Convertible. Not only was it a huge car, but he had bought it in Vancouver, after Her Majesty the Queen, had been driven in it on her tour of Canada when she was still our Princess. On the dashboard was a small gold plate inscribed with words that confirmed this. George pointed out to me the rack in front that had held a gun.

You can imagine the feeling I had when George asked me if I would drive him and his sister-in-law to Scotland on a holiday. Here was I, a kid born to working-class people, about to drive the car in which our Queen had ridden in. I couldn't believe that it was happening. The only thing that troubled me was the fact that on our small country roads, this car took up almost three-quarters of them and the steering wheel was on the left-hand side of the car. Anyway I wasn't going to miss a chance like that, so in June away we went.

All went well until we approached Lancaster and there was a slight drizzle of rain. We had kept pretty well to the quieter roads. Going up a hill, I felt the back end start to swing a little. Up over the rise I could see a small

English car coming towards us. As our car was so wide, I knew it was going to clip the other car if I wasn't careful. Sure enough, the back end caught his door and the impact was hard enough to send him into the ditch. I hit the curbstone and the front mudguard of our car bent inwards, jamming it against the wheel. Luckily there was a garage at the bottom of the hill that we had just driven by. Well, a lady got out of the car and George rolled down his window. He was a man of about 70 years old at this time I believe. Whilst her husband got out of their car to inspect the damage, she rushed over to George and went up one side of him and down the other. She was screaming and carrying on that he shouldn't be driving at his age in such a big car.

He let her yell for about five minutes and then lifted up his hands and said, "But Madam I have no wheel." If you'd have seen the look on her face… I had a hard time not to laugh. However, apparently they were on their way to catch the ferry to take them to France. George offered right then to give them £100 to get them to their destination but she turned him down. There was only slight damage to their car and we exchanged the necessary information. She insisted that the police be called so George told me to go right ahead I went down to the garage to 'phone for the police and after a short time, three different local 'Bobbies' arrived. One on a bike, one on a motorbike and the other in a small car (he was the sergeant). One went in their car, one got in with George, and I went into the police car with the sergeant.

Fortunately for me he was a great guy and when he saw my driving license he recognised my name. We talked about what had happened and he said that it was a bad road when wet and that a lot of accidents had occurred in that particular spot. This made me feel a bit better.

Anyway, we then talked about football for about 20 minutes and he told us he would have the car towed to the garage and perhaps they could fix the mudguard. I don't know what the lady was thinking when she wanted to call the police… perhaps she thought they were entitled to get more than the £100 that George had offered her. This was in no way intended to be a bribe. He just felt badly that their holiday had been delayed. Anyway, we never heard anything more of the incident afterwards. I have a feeling that two people were kicking themselves at a later date that they hadn't accepted George's offer, as in those days, £100 was considered to be quite a lot of money. I got a lot of ribbing from the team after I had told them all about it. Frank Broome said that he was surprised that I hadn't pressed charges against them for backing their door into my rear end.

During our tour of Scotland, George told me that Art, his son, was coming over to see me with the intention of offering me a job. He was looking for a manager for one of his hotels in Calgary and hoped I would consider the offer. I was 31 years old at the time and knew that my playing days wouldn't last forever, so I gave it some serious consideration. Art came over a few weeks later in August. He outlined what he had in mind and told me that he would find a house for us and that he would like me to start in the New Year. Jean and I never really discussed it at length. I somehow knew that it would be a good life for us out there. Having seen the place and having met several people, many of them English, I had a feeling that it would all work out.

At this time, I had been with the club for more than nine years and my second benefit would be due in May 1955. I could have stayed until then – took my benefit and left for Calgary. Instead, I asked to see the directors, told them of the situation and asked if I could be released from my contract. I was told on that day, that they would be sorry to lose me but they wished me well. I played my last game against Notts County at home. It was on 18 December and we drew 1-1. My old friend Lee Leuty was their captain at the time and as we shook hands at the end of the game, they played *Auld Lang Syne* over the loudspeakers. I had a lump in my throat and my wife in the stands had tears in her eyes. The fans gave me a great send off and I will never forget that day for as long as I live. I never did get my second benefit – not even half of it. After nine loyal years I received a cheque for £100.

A lot of books have been written over the years about Derby County and in them I have read items concerning me that had never happened. I was supposed to have asked for transfers many times – which I never did. I was supposed to have been suspended – which I never was. Rarely was I asked for facts before these books were writ-

My father-in-law Sid Dallison (left) pictured with my bar manager, Tom Campbell. Sid worked at Derby Loco Works for 40 years before joining us in Canada when he was in his 60s. He said he should have done it years ago!

ten so it is nice to have the opportunity of replying to these stories myself.

The incident with regard to my 'supposed' transfer to Sheffield can easily be explained. I was allowed to train there when my second daughter was born. This was in October of 1951. She was not expected to live and was taken to the Children's Hospital in Sheffield almost immediately after her birth. She stayed until she was almost a year old and for the first few weeks after her birth, I did my training on the Sheffield ground whilst visiting the hospital where my wife was with Lea. Of course the rumours were flying and it shows how easily they can start. Unless you hear football stories straight from the 'horse's mouth'… don't ever believe a word. I think all the members of the e-mail supporters clubs will agree with me on that. Right mates? We've had a few scares with 'hackers' getting on the line from time to time and starting some really juicy rumours.

25 December 1954 was the first year that I had been able to play 'Santa' to my daughters. Each year, since joining the club, we were always away for Christmas. Even if we were playing at home, we always had to go to the Midland Hotel so that we were together. Such were the rules and regulations in those days. However, I was to leave for Canada in January and the family was to follow in April. My wife was an only daughter and her parents had also decided to come with us. My father-in-law, Sidney Dallison, was my best friend and we always got along until the day he died ten years later. He also had been promised a job in the hotel so all was well. He was 62 years old at the time. It was a big change for both he and my mother-in-law but they soon settled in and both wished they had come out here to live earlier.

Calgary is a clean city with blue skies and sun almost all year round. It is very high above sea level so the air is excellent for anyone suffering from asthma. My mother-in-law had this problem and had never felt better after we had lived there for a short while. She lived until she was 82 years of age. Had she stayed in Derby, I doubt if she would have lasted as well.

I left England in January 1955 on board the *Empress of France* and landed in Halifax, Nova Scotia, five days later. Once again I was confined to my cabin, as I was seasick for the first couple of days. The journey to Calgary by train took three days. It was the middle of winter and all I could see out of the train window was snow, snow and more snow. I was glad when the train pulled in at the Calgary station and there Mr Davis was waiting to take me to his home. It was a bright sunny day and not a cloud in the sky. Snow was on the ground and I was told it would stay there until around April. The thing that impressed me most of all about Calgary was its wide streets, the sunshine and clear blue skies and the views of the mountains in the distance.

The next day I was taken to the hotel I was to manage which was in the downtown area. It didn't take long to get to know the staff and I settled in quickly. Those first few weeks were harder for the girls on the desk than they were for me because they had a hard time understanding my accent!

Jean's mum, Sarah Dallison, my mum, Edith Mozley, Jean, and daughters Lynne and Lea, all pictured outside the Hotel Royal during the Calgary Stampede days.

The Royal Hotel was noted for its yearly Indian costume parade. There are several Indian Reserves close to Calgary and each tribe would take part in a competition run by Mr Davis for the best hand-made outfit. Some of the beadwork on the costumes was very unusual and must have taken hours to sew by hand. Each tribe would enter the street in front of the hotel with the chief leading them on horseback. I remember feeling a real idiot that first year. I was supposed to take the winner and lead the horse to Mrs Davis who would then present the prize. Having previously explained that my only contact with 'horses' was on Blackpool beach, I somehow managed to get the bridle off this horse as I was trying to lead it towards Mrs Davis. Well, here I am struggling to put it back on with the chief laughing his head off at me. In the end, he dismounted and slipped it on without any problem. He looked at me and said, "I thought the English knew all about horses." I didn't like to say that this one had only watched them racing at Ascot on TV. My face was redder than the Mountie's coat (who was also having a grin at my expense) and I was glad to get that first year over and done with. All this was witnessed by hundreds of people watching the parade of costumes. I felt a right 'twit'.

Settling In

HAVING always been into fitness and a member of the Health and Strength organisation since the age of 14, I would go to one of the health clubs regularly to have my workouts. The one closest to the hotel belonged to a man by the name of Gordon Pogue. Gordon was one of the fittest men I have ever known. He lived, breathed and talked fitness to the many oil executives who had joined as members. Gordon was still swimming a mile in his late 60s, and after undergoing surgery for a heart problem in his late 70s, he was back on the running machine doing a mile exactly four weeks after the operation. At the hotel, we had many top-class wrestlers staying with us and I got to know them very well, as they would have a workout at Pogues too.

We would have a lot of laughs over coffee in the restaurant downstairs. I recall one night we were having a bit of trouble in one of the hotel rooms with a few young men having a noisy party. The girls on the desk had phoned and asked if they would keep the noise down but to no avail. I happened to be talking to two of the wrestling brothers at that time – The Miller Brothers – and they said, "Bert, we'll come with you up to the room if you like." Both of these men were 6ft 6ins tall. They weighed-in at around 18st each. We took the elevator up to the fourth floor and I knocked on the door. This happy young man opened the door and I told him I was the manager of the hotel and would they please keep the noise down. By this time his friends had also come to the door and after taking one look at the wrestlers – I got an apology and we left. We never heard a peep out of them for the rest of the night.

Mr Stu Hart (whose son Owen was tragically killed in a recent accident in a World Federation wrestling match in the US), owned a wrestling circuit that took in Edmonton, Regina and Calgary. Some of those men who wrestled for him were huge and made me look like a 7st weakling. I would often invite some of them over to the house so that they could relax in a garden instead of just the four walls of the hotel. I have many pictures of them, as you can see, and they all had a sense of humour that matched my own. In later years my daughter, Lynne, would baby-sit the Hart children. Can you imagine having nine boys and three girls? When they were young, they were all very strong and would wrestle with each other in the basement of their house which was made into a gym.

Mr and Mrs Hart did a wonderful job raising their

I'm wearing my six-gallon hat and pictured with hotel guests during the Calgary Stampede.

family. Stu wouldn't allow them to eat chocolate except perhaps at Easter time. As he said to me at one time, "Bert, can you imagine the dentist's bill if all 13 had to go each year for major fillings?" Over here at that time, there was not a Government medical plan and hospital and dentists' fees were very high.

When exercising at Pogues, I met several men who were interested in bodybuilding. They had contests at the YMCA on occasions and I was persuaded to enter in some of these. I was lucky to take home several trophies during the time that I was in Calgary. I came first in the Mr Calgary contest – winning the Best Arms and Best Legs; held the Odd Lift championship for Alberta from 1960 until just two years ago; and came second and third in several other meets in and around the Province.

I would urge any youngster, to take up bodybuilding as soon as they reach their teens. Building up the mus-

cles with lightweight exercises in repetition, on a regular basis will help to promote a healthy body. *Never*, on any account, resort to steroids. I have seen the damage it has done to some of the weightlifters over here, men who wanted to grow big muscles the easy way. Many young men have lost their lives to cancer, as I am sure they have in England too. I have never taken any artificial stimulants in my life and would urge any aspiring athlete to follow this rule.

I met many of the professional footballers and hockey players during my stay at Pogues gym. It took the Americans quite a while to get used to my accent but when they did I would get a lot of good-natured teasing. I remember getting my own back on the class one morning. I would take them for a mat routine and have them lying facing me. On this particular morning, as they waited for me to start the first exercise, I said, "Oh, just a minute guys. I need to change a few of you around." So I said, "Herm, will you go over there on the back row –

play the piano and I just wanted to see what the notes looked like." We had several black American players with the Calgary Stampeder Football club so I had arranged them on the mats to look like the scale. They all had a good laugh and I found many black friends who had a sense of humour such as my own.

One, a man named Herm Harrison, was a top player with the Calgary Stampeders Football Club. He was a huge man, well-built and a lot of fun. We would have coffee together most mornings and one day during the summer I hadn't seen him for a few days as they had been playing away from Calgary. It had been really hot so I greeted him in my own way with, "Hi Herm – by heck you've been out in the sun haven't you – what a great tan you've got this year." Herm was, of course, black to start with. Not to be outdone, he said, "Yes Bert, I tried out that new sun-tan lotion they were advertising." We both had straight faces and the people within hearing distance kept looking at each other and then looking away, trying to be polite and yet wondering what on earth we were talking about.

In the 1950s, there was still a section of the public who was prejudiced. They were mostly Americans who worked with the oil companies and who had lived in the Southern States, One or two hotels would not accept reservations from anyone, who was black, in case they lost the business of their many US customers. I was delighted

and you Bob come down here in the middle." This went on until I had switched about eight of them. They couldn't figure out what was going on and after they were all settled I said, "Right – I've been learning how to

Christmas greetings from Stu Hart and family. Stu owned a wrestling circuit and they used our hotel.

Yours truly pictured with some of the wrestlers who stayed at our Calgary hotel.

one day to receive a 'phone call from someone trying to make a reservation for Mr Louis Armstrong, his wife and the members of his band. They had tried to get rooms at the large CPR (Canadian Pacific Railroad) Hotel but had been told they were fully booked. I reserved a suite on the top floor for them and they booked for the week that they were in concert. I had breakfast with him and his wife and spent a very enjoyable hour listening to his stories. He gave me tickets to his concert and I couldn't have wished for nicer people as guests in the hotel. On the night they were to leave, his band had assembled in the lobby and the girls on the desk asked them to play a tune for them, as

they had been unable to attend the concert. They instantly obliged and, to the delight of staff and guests alike, an impromptu concert was given right there on the spot.

We had many well-known sports personalities stay at the hotel during the years that I was the manager. These included many of the top world-class wrestlers, the Harlem Globe Trotters, a Japanese Olympic ice hockey team, several English First Division football teams – Tottenham, West Brom, Birmingham – one of the Russian touring teams and last but not least, Jersey Joe Walcott who was the heavyweight boxing champion of the world. I am very lucky to have met so many of the world 'greats' and have lots of souvenirs that are reminders of this time in my life.

Among some of the entertainers in show business, who stayed with us at the hotel, were the Ames Brothers who were very popular in the 1960s. They were a singing group and made many records and movies during their career. One day Joe, who was the oldest in the group, asked me if I would give him a work- out if he came to the gym with me. I fixed him up with some gym kit and took him to Pogues. Showing him a routine, I told him just to take it easy the first time. However, Ed, his younger brother, came to me the next day and said that Joe was so stiff he could hardly walk up the steps to the stage. His other brothers really gave him a bad time for trying to 'show off' his muscles and keep up with me.

Many of you have probably heard of the Calgary Stampede and in fact have no doubt seen the chuck wagon races on TV. It is an event that lasts around two weeks and always in July. They invite a celebrity to take part in the opening ceremony and as the publicity is usually second to none, seldom does the Stampede board get a refusal. Some of the personalities that I have met include Gene Barry (Bat Masterson in films), the Cisco Kid and his partner Pancho, who was a real happy character, Johnny Cash and his wife June. I also met Gracie Fields who was touring Canada at the time when I was in Toronto.

I was delighted one day at the Royal Hotel, to receive a booking from Norman Evans. Perhaps some of our

The author with Dr Bill Miller, one of the Miller wrestling brothers, and some costume winners during the Calgary Stampede days.

older generation would remember Norman. He would do his skit called 'Over The Garden Wall'. I knew Norman from the time he came to Derby to appear at the Hippodrome in Green Lane and when I knew he was booked to perform in Calgary, I went to meet him in at the CPR station. He was with a concert party of about 18 others and I was able to put on a dinner for him and the cast late one night after they had finished their show. Norman really appreciated this as in Canada usually the restaurants closed down after nine o'clock and they hadn't been able to all sit down to dinner together, since leaving England.

Ouch! Wrestler Lou Thez gets to grips with me.

However, the lady who appreciated it even more than Norman was another great entertainer from the vaudeville days, Tessie O'Shea. Tessie was from Manchester and told me that she knew Henry Rose, who was the sports journalist killed in the plane that crashed in Munich, carrying the Manchester United football team in 1958. Tessie told me that she was heart-broken to hear of Henry's death, as he had been a very dear friend She also told me that he used to push her in her pram as he lived near to where she was born. I heard from her several times after this meeting and she later left England and went to live in New York where she appeared on several American shows, including the *Ed Sullivan Show*. Norman told me that he was due to play at Derby Hippodrome the month after he returned to England and he promised he would pass on my greetings to the Derby audience that week. My sister attended the show and he kept his word.

Life in Canada was very different from the way of life I had left behind in England. I remember the first week that I arrived in Calgary. I stayed with the Davis family until I could get accommodation for my family and on that first weekend, they told me they would take me to Banff for a picnic. When I asked where Banff was, I was told 'about 90 miles west'. My idea of a picnic was to take a few sandwiches to Markeaton Park and feed the ducks. As time went by, it got to 1 o'clock – then 2 o'clock – then 3 o'clock and I kept wondering when they were going to start on this 90-mile trip. I had pictured winding roads like England and about a three-hour trip. Instead, we left at 4 o'clock and were eating hot dogs and hamburgers by half-past five in Banff.

In the heart of the mountains, Banff is a beautiful winter resort as well as a summer playground and many

Pictured outside our hotel with more costume winners.

US wrestling champion Tony Rocca wrote me this special message, 'To my good friend, Bert Mozley'.

I won this Alberta Olympic competition. With me are Joe Stockinger (centre) and Bob Develin.

With some of my bodybuilding trophies, not forgetting my England caps.

well-known celebrities usually stay at the Banff Springs Hotel. The hotel is made from stone blocks and just looks like a medieval castle. A great golf course is at the back of the grounds and hot sulphur springs complete the picture. The highway was divided and pretty straight all the way, Mr Davis had no problem reaching a comfortable 90 miles an hour in his Cadillac and as I said before, we had a fire going and ate our supper by 5.30pm that day.

Tessie O'Shea became a great friend of ours.

The Japanese Olympic ice hockey team were guests at our hotel in Calgary.

Chatting to some old adversaries when West Brom visited Canada. England star Ronnie Allen is on the extreme right of the picture.

The Austrian visitors of Admira Wien.

With Jersey Joe Walcott, world heavyweight boxing champion (on my immediate left).

Bat Masterson (alias Gene Barry) tries to tip my hat.

With Norman Evans of *Over The Garden Wall* fame. He passed on my best wishes to the people of Derby when he returned to England to appear at the Hippodrome in Green Lane.

With Jean and Dr and Mrs Salisbury from Iowa, who were guests at our Banff Springs Hotel.

Previous page: I shake hands with the Cisco Kid.

Playing Soccer Again

THE first year that I was in Calgary, I was asked to join the Caledonian Soccer Club. This team, as the name implies, consisted of Scots who had emigrated to Canada over the years. I had to obtain permission from the FA and was granted an amateur status. If I should return to England to play, I would automatically belong to Derby County again. There were about five teams in the area and they were mostly ethnic groups. Italian, German, Croatian and Hungarian. The soccer was rough and ready and took me back to the old days of Shelton United. However, it was fun and I was lucky not to get clobbered a time or two from some of the tackles. I was also asked to try out with the Calgary Stampeders Football Club as a place kicker. In fact I was the first 'soccer style kicker' ever to have a try-out. I was able to kick the ball easily between the posts but that year, the Stampeders had a full team and as I was classed as an import I couldn't be signed. Now, almost every American Football team has a soccer player as their place kicker. All he does, as perhaps you know, is to run on to the field to kick a field goal.

That summer, the Russian touring team came to Toronto and I was picked to join the Canadian team. I had not met any of the officials of the Canadian Football Association, as they were all living in Toronto, 3,000 miles away from Calgary. Professional football did not exist in Canada at that time and I noticed that most of the other members of the team were just young boys in college. When the team was posted, I was not selected to play and one of the players, named Joe Johnson from Scotland, asked me if I was injured. When I said that I wasn't, he went to the officials to ask why I was not included. He was told that they thought, as I was 31 years old, that I was 'over the hill'.

Well, the Russians played their usual game and I felt sorry for the young left-back. The winger had him beat every time and all the danger was coming from that side. Anyway, at half-time, Canada was losing and I guess the officials must have had second thoughts because they came and asked me to get stripped off to play in the left-back position. I told them that if I was over the hill in the first half – I hadn't suddenly become rejuvenated to play in the second. Anyway, to help the team out I decided to play. In the second half, I was able to stop the Russian winger each time he tried to race me down the wing and no more goals were scored from that side. After the

Bert Mozley, ex-Derby County and England, now coach to the Calgary Police Department soccer team.

The Caledonian Soccer Club, for whom I played for and coached.

game, the Russian officials came over to me and wanted to talk. I must have made an impression as they were asking me questions about the best method of playing defence. They wanted me to explain to their full-backs how to play against a fast winger. I often wondered where their interpreter was educated as he spoke perfect 'Queen's English'.

In 1960 a second Russian team came to Canada. They hadn't been beaten in the 60 previous games that they had played in. At that time I was coaching and also playing in the Calgary All-Star team that was to meet them. As the Russian team came across Canada, playing in each Province, we noticed that they were winning all their games comfortably. I told my team not to worry but to just play the game to the best of their ability. It was a beautiful summer evening and they played well above themselves. We were winning by one goal and near to the end the opposition was attacking time after time. I don't know how we kept them out. These young men from Russia were brilliant athletes. Our team consisted of players who worked during the week and played for the love of the game each Saturday. However they played their hearts out and we were all just about on our knees when that final whistle went. We had achieved what no other team in Canada had done. We had beaten the Russians!

Now I will tell you about the time I played a joke on one of the RCMP's (Royal Canadian Mounted Police). There was an outing planned for the Russians the day after the match. We were going to take them to Banff for the day. There was at that time, what was referred to as 'the Cold War' between the Soviet Union and the

The Russian centre-forward gets in a shot against Calgary All Stars.

Bert Mozley on the scoresheet. I find the back of the net against the Russians. We won 4-1, the only team to beat them on their tour.

in particular who they suspected of being a spy. We arrived at Banff and took the team on a tour of the town by bus. Afterwards, we all went to a hotel for a meal. I sat next to the policeman and as he leaned over to me he whispered, "Bert, where's Blondie?" I kept my face straight and said "Oh he left in a taxi about five minutes ago." I thought he was going to have a fit right on the spot. He jumped up and said, "Where did he go?" and then saw me starting to laugh. He called me all the names under the sun – most of which I can't print – but he saw the funny side of it later.

I stayed as manager of the Royal and the Wales Hotels until 1962 when Mr Davis decided to retire from the hotel business. He sold his chain to another company who brought in their own staff. At this point I was out of a job. However, I had heard that Mr Pogue

Western Powers. A special agent from the police department was in plain clothes and was to accompany the team wherever they went. He was marking just one man needed an assistant at his health club and I applied and got the position. I loved that job and stayed with him until he also sold and left to retire in Hawaii.

The Russians wave goodbye before leaving.

Each year, during the summer months, an English touring team would come over and play in Calgary. We would invite them to our home to have a barbecue, which gave them a night away from their hotels. One year, as I previously mentioned, it was the Birmingham side and another year Tottenham came. I recall the year that West Brom arrived and my wife had been making home-made wine. It was pretty potent stuff and a couple of the players wished the next morning that they had stayed with milk!

I was able to play in the representative matches until I was well past 40 years of age. My gym has many of the pennants on display, presented to me by these different teams who played in Alberta. However, I couldn't beat the

Soccer coach to the Atco Industries team.

Sir Stanley Matthews arrives in Toronto.

Our daughter, Lea, with Sir Stanley on an afternoon stroll through Calgary.

playing record of Sir Stanley Matthews. Stan visited Canada in 1962 and came to Alberta and British Columbia for a few days. He visited me and we had a great time catching up on all the things that had hap-pened since we were on tour together in 1950. The stories that man can tell are so interesting, I only wish that one day a movie would be made depicting his life story.

It was in 1963 that in my spare time I would help to

With my old pal Sir Stanley Matthews. I first met Stan when I was still a young lad, when he played for Stoke City. Little did I realise that one day I'd play against him and then in the same England side, and that he'd become a good friend.

coach the Atco Industries soccer team. Atco manufactures large sleeping units that accommodate workers when they are out in the camps working on oil rigs. Mr Ron Southern, who was the president, had donated funds to encourage the game and at the same time to keep his employees fit. As Jean was making the curtains for them I had got to know many of their office managers. One friend asked what the chances were of getting a top English player to come over and play with a representative side. I had been in contact with Stan and

A happy group. Left to right are: Vic Arelis, Jerry Grande, Sir Stanley Matthews, Sid Slater, Derek McCorquindale (the tall man), Jack Buckler, Bert Mozley and Bob Barbosa.

Sir Stan, complete with white Stetson, is about to be interviewed by local TV in Calgary.

decided to ask him if he would consider coming over to play with our team at the McMahon Stadium. He agreed and in July of that year we greeted him at the Calgary Airport. The local Alberta FA had arranged all the matches and we were to play in Edmonton and the following week in Calgary.

At Edmonton, the opposition consisted of mostly amateur players. One or two were from Europe and knew a little more about the game than the Canadian boys. Stan was given a great reception. The full-back playing against him was trying his best but was going head-on into tackles with Stan. As it was supposed to be an exhibition game, Stan didn't get annoyed with the guy but after half-time, we agreed that he should give this lad a lesson in football. Well, Stan turned it on… he played picture book football and the lad didn't know which way to turn each time Stan got the ball. The crowd loved it. However, on the following Sunday, we

were all stripped and ready to play and the bus bringing this same team from Edmonton, didn't arrive. A quick 'phone call confirmed our worst fears. They hadn't even left. I do not know to this day what excuse was given to the organisers but I do remember the five very happy men in the stands who one day, would be able to tell their grandchildren that they had played in a team against Sir Stanley Matthews. We were able to field our reserves and then make up a team from spectators who had come to watch the game. The crowd in the stands didn't mind it at all as they had only come to see one man. This shows the kind of man, Sir Stanley Matthews was and is – he gave his all that afternoon and played alongside a team of total amateurs making them feel ten feet tall.

The same week that Stan arrived, the Calgary Stampede was taking place. Each year, a famous personality is chosen to lead the parade. This particular year, Gordie Howe of the Detroit Red Wings hockey team was the Parade Marshall. Gordie at that time was as highly-regarded in

Introducing Sir Stan to an inspector with the Calgary police force.

his sport as Stan was in football. During an interview, Gordie was asked by the press how he had managed to play hockey for such a long time (he was around 40 years old I believe). Turning to Stan, he said, "I think you should ask this gentleman that question – he has been playing his sport for a lot longer than I have."

Stan received many compliments that summer. One day we met Rocky Marciano, the world heavyweight

Sir Stan with myself and Atco manager Jerry Grande.

boxing champion. When he was introduced to Stan and was told that he was still playing football it wasn't long before he was asking Stan which was the best way to breathe. Afterwards, both Stan and I thought how unusual it was for him not to know how to breathe properly when he was already a world champion. It wasn't too long after this that Stan was invited to Toronto to play for Toronto City and he stayed there for many years. On his 70th birthday, I was invited to Toronto where a party was to be given in his honour. Unfortunately, I had just come out of hospital after having a detached retina and was unable to go.

The Good Life

AFTER Mr Pogue left the city, I went to work for the International Hotel as their health director. They had a nice gym within the hotel with sauna and pool and a good mat area for weights. Doing the thing that I loved to do each day was my ideal way of life. My wife had a thriving drapery business and we managed to buy a small log cabin and an acre of land out at Bragg Creek near Calgary. It bordered on the river and we spent many happy weekends with our daughters and their friends, while they were growing up. This was just a summer cottage suitable for a get-a-way but it was a very healthy way to spend our holidays, catching and cooking trout for breakfast on many occasions from out of the river that flowed at the bottom of the garden. The only thing we had to look out for, once out

An idyll...our log cabin at Bragg Creek.

of the cities were the bears. They would be drawn to the smell of food and we have had to pack away our groceries and retreat to the car several times during those 19 years that we spent in Alberta.

It was at this time that I was asked if I would like to try refereeing wrestling matches. They were held every Friday night in the Stampede grounds and drew a crowd of about 2,000 people. Stu Hart was the promoter, as I mentioned before. I knew him very well as he previously booked the wrestlers in to stay at the hotel when I was the manager there. Although I had never wrestled before, Stu told me that it would be easy for me to referee. I was still

quite agile on my feet and could skip out of danger if it presented itself. Famous last words? During the two or three years that I did referee, I had my nose broken twice, stitches in my head and was knocked out of the ring and landed on the concrete floor.

Although wrestling is a good entertaining sport, many times tempers do get frayed and real punches are landed. It doesn't happen often as they are all the best of friends but there are occasions when they do get hurt and have to go to hospital to be treated. I made many friends and they were always ready for a laugh and a joke, as you with will see from some of the photographs. On

I've turned my hand to many things over the years and here I'm refereeing a wrestling match.

one occasion, I met Primo Carnera, the Italian heavyweight boxing champion. I have never before seen a man with such big feet. I recall someone saying that if ever he was shot, somebody would have to push him over to get him to lie down.

That same year, Mantovani and his Orchestra came to Calgary. Stu Hart wanted to go to the concert but wasn't able to get tickets. I knew one of the members of the band and was able to get a couple of tickets, so Stu and I went together. Someone must have told Mantovani that I was an ex-Derby County player as he sent word through Wally, his band manager, that he would like to meet me afterwards in his dressing room. As this was a gala event, many of the ladies in the audience had dressed very formally in evening gowns, and were waiting backstage with their husbands, hoping to meet the great man himself. Stu and I, dressed very casually, joined the throng and were rather looked down on by the rest of this well-dressed group.

The door of Mantovani's room opened and a man came out and said, "Would Mr Bert Mozley please step forward." Stu and I went to the front of the line and were ushered inside. We had a great visit with this gentleman and I still have the autographed album he gave to me that night. I think if looks could have killed as we stepped in front of the queue to go inside, I wouldn't be writing this now. The following day was a Sunday, so I asked those in the band who were free if they would like to come home with me for a barbecue. I think about five

of them came and once again, Jean's homemade wine was sampled. Two of them fell asleep in the lawn chairs and we had to waken them to drive them back to the hotel. We tested that wine one day and found it to be 16 per cent proof; after that I always stayed with a shandy. My sister also sampled it on one occasion when she was visiting. It was September and before the night was over, she was singing the Christmas carol, *Silent Night* in German I don't know how she did it in German, as she doesn't speak English all that well! I won't say any more Beryl.

As perhaps many of you know, Canada is noted for its salmon. The first time we decided to go fishing for salmon was in September 1965. Our friends had a small boat and had left to go to Lake Shuswap in British Columbia. We had decided to join them a couple of days later and as we drove into the motel which was on the side of the Lake, Art, our friend, was just pulling in to tie up the boat. It had been raining so I slipped on my 'wellies' and went down to the shoreline to help him. Thinking that the lake was shallow at the edge, I decided to step in as I had my 'wellies' on, so that I could reach the rope that he was holding. The next thing I knew, I was up to my chin in water. It had been dredged, of course, to allow boats with deep hulls to come right in to shore. I thought my friends would never stop laughing. That was a good start to our holiday, it took three days for my jacket to fully dry! Luckily for me, Art had a spare coat that I was able to borrow. We took out the boat the

My farewell night with hotel staff before leaving Alberta for British Columbia.

following morning and started to troll. I sat on one side of the boat with my rod and Jean sat on the other. She got the first strike and reeled in a 25lb salmon. It was a beauty. Not long afterwards… zing – her rod went again.

Meanwhile I hadn't even had a bite. For three days we did this. Both had the same lures – both had the same rods – fished out of the same boat – but Jean caught all the fish and I was there just to haul them in. We took home over 80lbs of salmon that week and before the winter was over we were fed up with eating it! We later bought a boat ourselves after we moved to Victoria and it was always the same – Jean would catch the fish and I'd be the one cleaning them. Never did like fishing!

We had often talked of moving to the coast where it was a bit warmer in the winters, and in 1972, we decided to do just that. Our daughters were by this time both married and our friends had already moved there and were writing letters telling us how lovely it was. We decided to put our house on the market and in no time it was sold. We loaded up the car, put the dog in the back and set off to drive the 500 odd miles to our new city. The furniture was in storage and as soon as we had found a house we would call them to deliver it. The drive through the Rockies was great and we finally came to the Pacific Ocean. It was the first time we had both been that far west together and Jean liked the look of Victoria as soon as we saw it. It is nicknamed 'the city of flowers' with good reason. Hanging baskets of all colours are on every lamppost down town and each garden is a joy to see. They have competitions for the best gardens and it must be really hard to choose a winner. It didn't take long for us to find a house and we were lucky enough to have a view of the Pacific Ocean.

I was almost 50 years old and still had to work for 15 years before I would receive my pension. At that time, there was lots of work available and within two days I had the offer of two jobs. One was in a gym in downtown

The BC Ferries vessel which takes us to Galiano Island.

Victoria and the other to teach soccer at Royal Roads Military College. I chose the latter, even though it was only part-time, and had a lot of fun with the young men who were all officer cadets. During the time that I was coaching them, I was able to use all the facilities of the college. This included the swimming pool, sergeants' mess – where each Saturday night they held a get-together – and, of course, the dining room. Some of the meals the cooks prepared were out of this world and we only had to pay just a small amount as I was treated as staff.

During this time, I took the cadets down to Colorado (where Derby County played a US representative side recently). Unfortunately Derby lost that game but I can

Home sweet home...Galiano Island, a million miles from Chester Green – but I still love the old town!

understand why as Denver, the city they played in, is a mile above sea level. The air is quite thin and if you are not used to it, it can tire you very quickly.

At this time I was offered a job to coach the American cadets there but Jean didn't want to live in the US so I turned it down. I was with Royal Roads College for two years and then I heard of a job going on Galiano Island. It was to manage the small golf course there. Jean and I went for an interview and got the job. Luckily for us, it was a sellers' market and in three days our house in Victoria was sold.

Galiano is the first island you pass on the ferry when

Signing my contract to coach Royal Roads Military College.

Royal Roads Military College soccer team. In case you're wondering, I'm the young man on the extreme right of the back row.

leaving Vancouver to get to Victoria. We arrived in November, not really sure of everything that the job would entail. After dealing with a staff of over 50 people at the Royal Hotel, it seemed strange that just Jean and the groundskeeper plus myself were the only employees of this little golf club. During the winter months it closed so we had three months holiday. The members were mostly retired but some lived on the mainland in Vancouver and had summer cottages. One or two would commute each day from Galiano. They were mostly the people who were taking courses at the University. We found life very peaceful there. No crime, as there was no way to get off the island other than on the ferry. In fact we only had a policeman for three months in the summer and the locals would laugh and talk about their 'rent-a-cop'. There is just one road going to the north end of the island, a distance of 19 miles. At its widest point it is just over five miles.

Kisses for one of Lea's pets, a young deer.

Our younger daughter, Lea, decided to come to live on the island too, and later married a man who was born here. Her 'family' now consists of cats, deer and stray dogs. In fact anything on four legs that needs a home she will take in. I visited her home the other night to find five deer waiting outside her back door. The doe had her baby with her and it still had spots showing. This is quite unusual as normally they keep their fawns hidden for many weeks. There are three generations that respond to

Going fishing…off for the day.

their names when she calls them. 'Apples, Pine-apple and Crab-apple.' Her husband, Bill, is quite relieved that there aren't elephants living in this region! Otherwise she'd be feeding them in the garden too!

Waiting for a bite!

Jean proudly shows off her 25lbs salmon at Lake Shuswap.

There were about 120 members at the Galiano Golf and Country Club and quite a challenging nine-hole course. Friday night was our busiest night and I organised a darts match each week, which went over really well. A few of the English people had played before and soon we had teams lined up and a really good-natured rivalry taking place between the 'lads' and the 'lasses'. After enjoying several years there, it was time to go back to Derby for a well-earned holiday. This proved to be something extra special, thanks to my wife's sister-in-law, Mary Dallison.

Still cleaning and not catching!

Happy Reunions

BACK in Derby, Mary Dallison had decided to surprise us and had asked Tommy Powell and Reg Harrison to try to contact as many of my old teammates as possible and she would give a garden party for us at her home in Littleover. Thinking we were just going over to her house for tea, can you imagine the surprise we got to find Frank Broome and his wife Elsie, who had come all the way from Ottery St Mary, in Devon, Jack Stamps and Nora from Burton upon Trent, Tim and Nancy Ward, who also lived close to that area, Reg and Wyn Harrison, Ted and Fran Robshaw, Tommy Powell and to put the icing on the cake for Jean, Ruby Musson who was over on holiday at the time from Australia. We had a wonderful day. It was the first time we had seen Frank, Elsie and Ruby since we left England in 1955.

Did someone say the Three Stooges? With dear pals Reg Harrison and Tommy Powell.

The passing years had made a difference to us all but the old magic when we all got talking together was still there. The years rolled away and we were back in 1948, talking of that FA Cup that we came so close to getting when we lost in the semi-final against Manchester United. In all the visits I have made to England, this was the one that I will never forget. It was the last time that I saw Jack and Nora, who both died within weeks of each other, and also Frank, Tim and Nancy who passed away a few years later. Our thanks go to Mary for such a wonderful gesture. She made a lot of people very happy that day.

One of my more recent visits to Derby, in 1997, was

Happy reunion in Derby. Frankie Broome is on my right, Reg Harrison on my left. Jack and Nora Stamps are extreme right of the front row. Long distance runner Lew Patrick is on the ground next to my twin sister, Beryl.

also a very special one. Pride Park was the talk of the Premier League and thanks to Mr Lionel Pickering, I was able to see it in all its glory. Never have I seen such a magnificent facility. When I think of the old Baseball Ground, it was like comparing night to day.

I was very grateful to Mr Pickering as he gave me tickets to attend two of the games and also allowed my granddaughter Samantha and her husband to accompany me. I was also presented with an up-to-date Derby County shirt with my old number-two on the back of it.

From left to right: Frankie Broome, Jack Stamps, yours truly, Reg Harrison and Ted Robshaw.

Lunch with ex-England star Neil Franklin at Ashbourne.

Tim and Nancy Ward when we visited them at Barton under Needwood.

This will be treasured always. It was the first time any of my grandchildren had witnessed an English football game and their cheers and chants of "D-E-R-B-Y" preceded by the claps were the loudest of all in our section.

As I watched the game, my thoughts went back 50 years and I wondered how the present players would fare in our heavy boots, playing with heavy ball on the muddy pitch at the Baseball Ground. I know the distinct advantage would be to the players of my era. With the light ball that is used today, I think both our half-backs and for that matter full-backs, would be taking shots from the halfway line and scoring.

Comparing this new method of play, I noticed that it seems to be a 'one-touch' game. In our day, we had players with individual skills who would dribble or body swerve past the opposition when heading for the goal. Now it seems that the idea is to pass the ball as quickly as possible to anyone wearing the same coloured shirt.

Proudly showing off the new Rams shirt given to me by Lionel Pickering after the opening of Pride Park Stadium.

Even from the halfway line back to the goalkeeper on many occasions. How times change indeed. I also remember that when a goal was scored, we would give a handshake or a pat on the back to the player. He did the job that he was paid to do. Now, the scorer is often injured by his own teammates who take a flying leap on to his back. I have often wondered why the trainers of the teams haven't put a stop to this. With the transfer fees being so high, an injury could mean the loss of a great deal of money if that player sustained a severe back injury that ended his career.

Reg Harrison tells me that since Mr Lionel Pickering took over the club, he has recognised the old players in a way that none of the other chairmen did who came before him. There is a special place reserved each home game for any 'ex-Ram' who wishes to attend.

After the game a refreshment room is available where they can chat with others who are guests of the day. It made me very happy to be able to meet, apart from Reg, Norman Nielson, Jim Bullions, Jeff Knight and Angus Morrison that afternoon. My granddaughter and her husband still talk of the occasion and of the players I was able to introduce them to. One of the highlights of the day was when Mr Pickering told me that I was one of his 'heroes' when he watched me play 50 years ago. It made that cramped 12-hour plane trip worthwhile and I thanked him for the compliment. It's nice to know that you are not forgotten especially when that 'someone' is the chairman of Derby County Football Club. I look back with pride and feel privileged that I once wore the white number-two shirt.

Guess who? Me or Rammy?

Where I scored a goal against Birmingham City's Gil Merrick at the Baseball Ground all those years ago.

My old peg at the Baseball Ground.

This holiday was the first time that my grandson-in-law had been to England. His passion was taking car engines to pieces and putting them back together again in his spare time. When I asked a friend, Cliff Haddock, who worked with me at Rolls-Royce in the pre-war years, if there was any chance of a tour of the factory, he set the ball in motion. Thanks to him and the people who showed us around the Rolls Royce Experimental Dept at Sinfin, we had a great afternoon. Not only did we see many different projects under way but also were both presented with a plaque to take home at the end of the day. Mike, my grandson-in-law, has never stopped talking about it as Rolls-Royce is a name that is treated with great respect in both Canada and the USA.

And Finally...

RECENTLY, my wife decided she wanted to get a computer. Our daughters and granddaughters have them and the 'phone bills are usually quite high each month with all the long-distance calls they make to each other. It didn't take her long after getting a computer, to find the Ramsnet and we have since made a lot of new 'cyber' friends from all parts of the world. (The 'phone bill is now almost non-existent too, thank goodness.) It really surprised me to find the enormous support given to the Rams by people who are living overseas – Australia, South Africa, Bermuda and just about every country in Europe look to the Ramsnet for news of their home team. Many of these supporters travelled hundreds of miles by 'plane or car to watch the games in Chicago and in Colorado, when Derby made their recent visit to the United States. I believe some members accompanied the team from Derby, too, and a lot of good natured notes were sent to these people asking if they'd bring a bottle of a favourite brew and a few meat pies with them. In fact we put a note in ourselves asking if they could make a detour via Galiano Island and drop off a couple for us. Those Derby meat pies take a lot of beating.

The latest bulletin put out over the net by one of the Belper lads, Stuart Hughes, is an invitational challenge to all Ramsnetters to forecast how the teams in the Premier League will finish at the end of the season. Jean and I have made out our lists and registered them with Stuart and we have a $10.00 bet as to who will come the closest. My life won't be worth living if she wins.

We were recently made honorary members of the North American Branch of the Derby County Supporters Club, which was formed by Jeff Willits, Dave Ottewell and Garry Archer a few years ago (who are all ex-patriots from Derby and surrounding districts). These men are devoted fans and give many hours of their time to keep interest alive for those so far from Pride Park. Since joining this happy band, I have met Pip White and his Dad who now live in Victoria close to my granddaughter. We spent a very enjoyable hour a week or two ago, having a coffee and talking about the Rams. It was nice to meet Pip and to put a face to a name that I had only seen on the computer. I would advise anyone who is a Ram's supporter and who has a computer, to join the Ramsnet and take part in the friendly banter that takes place each day on the line. More work for Nick but don't think he'll mind.

Jean and I have had more laughs at some of the exchanges that take place. The topic is, of course, the one and only Rams, mixed up with a few of the 'pleasantries'

My new charges, the Galiano School soccer team.

about our local opposition teams. Last year, I exchanged e-mails with a football fan in Vancouver. His team was Sunderland and I smiled when I received an e-mail this year saying that now Sunderland are in the Premier League, our friendship might not be as warm as it was last year. Derek – if we beat Sunderland I promise not to rub it in too much. And after our home drubbing back in September, I can't really can I?

We have also made many lasting friends over the years that were members of our golf club. I retired ten years ago. I say 'retired' but some days I work harder than I used to in my working days. I converted the double

Work out for a guest at my gym on Galiano Island.

Some of the first members of my gym on Galiano Island.

Gym member Ian Hooley, an over-50s champion.

garage where we live, into a gym and I now have about 30 people who come to train regularly with me. The youngest is 18 and the oldest 82. One man, Ian Hooley, is the Canadian triathalon champion in the over-50s group. He swims in the ocean just in front of my house, bikes up the 19 miles of hills and valleys here on the island and then runs for six miles to the gym from his home. He works out most days in the gym and has beaten men in the races he enters who are half his age. Since coming to the island, I have also helped to coach some of the schoolchildren here too. They had very little in the way of soccer 20 years ago but now there are four teams playing both male and female, and some of the girls are just as good as the guys.

Jean and I never had a son but I have always been very proud of my two daughters. I didn't have a grandson either – just two lovely granddaughters. When my granddaughter Meghan was expecting her first baby, I

A future Ram? Proud great-granddad with Markeith William Mozley Thonger.

Mozley Thonger, was born. I hope I can live long enough to teach him a little about the game of football. It will make a change now, when we go shopping, to look for football boots instead of ballet slippers! I hope I can pass down to him some of the genes that have helped me to enjoy a great life in sport.

Keeping fit has always been important to me. I look at some of the wages offered to the players today and shake my head. Back then, as a youth, I strived to make the grade for the honour of playing for my local team. The thought of money wasn't even there. Now football, to many, is just a game of 'pounds and pence'. It would seem that it's not what you can give to the game but what you can take from it.

I look back on my life and remember all those lasting friendships. Reg Harrison and I keep in touch to this day. Each time we meet in Derby we go over all the old times and revive the memories that we helped to make. I can honestly say, without a doubt in my mind, that I am glad that I played, when football was fun...

secretly hoped for a boy – but instead another beautiful girl, Miss Maddison Lynne Thonger, arrived.

However, a very special event in my life happened on 8 May 1999. My first great-grandson, Markeith William